Terry Bradshaw:
MAN OF STEEL
Terry Bradshaw with David Diles

Preface by Pete Rozelle

Foreword by Roger Staubach

OF THE ZONDERVAN CORPORATION
GRAND RAPIDS, MICHIGAN 49506

Cover photo by Heinz Kluetmeier for *Sports Illustrated*
Back cover photo by Bill Eppridge for *Sports Illustrated*
Cover design by Art Jacobs

TERRY BRADSHAW: MAN OF STEEL
Copyright © 1979, 1980 by The Zondervan Corporation
Grand Rapids, Michigan

Sixth printing 1980
This edition 1980

All rights reserved. No part of this publication may be reproduced, stored in a retrieval system, or transmitted in any form or by any means without the prior permission of the publisher.

Library of Congress Cataloging in Publication Data
Bradshaw, Terry.
    Terry Bradshaw, man of steel

    1. Bradshaw, Terry. 2. Football players—United States—Biography. 3. Pittsburgh Steelers (Football club) I. Diles, David L., joint author. II. Title.
GV939.B68A37   796.33'2'0924 [B]   79-16620
ISBN 0-310-39461-9

Printed in the United States of America

This book is dedicated to my parents, Novis and Bill Bradshaw, who provided a Christian home, thus giving me the finest environment in the world. By teaching me to care, to share, to believe in prayer and hard work, they prepared me for every struggle this life may put before me. Most of all, they gave me love.

—*Terry Bradshaw*

. . . and it is dedicated to Beverly Susan and David Lisle Diles, who have filled my cup to overflowing.

—*Dave Diles*

Contents

Statistical section follows page 206.

Acknowledgments

We are very grateful to a number of people who contributed generously, in a multitude of ways, in order that this book might become a reality.

Dr. David Allen gave guidance and wisdom in a most unselfish way. Rev. Jim Anderson, Fr. Jim Van Vurst, Dr. Bill Keucher, and Rev. Ed Libby provided lifts at a critical time.

The Bradshaw family opened homes and hearts. Members of the Pittsburgh Steeler family—the Rooneys, Chuck Noll, Joe Gordon, and members of the team—made us understand why they win so much.

Jack Finley and Ed Ahee always provide inspiration because they live their sermons.

The people at Louisiana Tech, Woodlawn High School, and Oak Terrace Junior High School gave willingly of their time, and Gerald Burnett gave wise counsel and valuable insight from the very start.

And Tom Wolfe provided common sense, as he always has done.

—*Dave Diles*

Preface

More and more, the role of the professional athlete in today's society is becoming quite complicated. His challenges do not restrict themselves to the playing field, where his opponent is easy to define. But they now often overlap into the player's private life, thus producing additional strains and pressures.

Young people's images of their favorite athletes now include more than game statistics. The player's life is never really private but, rightly or wrongly, is exposed to the scrutiny of his fans. This is especially difficult for the superstar.

On the following pages, author Dave Diles deals directly and candidly with one of the National Football League's true superstars and superheroes—Terry Bradshaw. Terry's record-setting performance in Super Bowl XIII was a fitting climax to an incredible season for the Pittsburgh Steelers and their quarterback. Pittsburgh is the only team to win three Super Bowls and, not by coincidence, Terry Bradshaw has been the quarterback each time.

But, as accomplished as Terry is on the playing field, it has been a peaks-and-valleys journey to the top for him. Being the first player chosen in the 1970 draft, immediate pressures were placed on Terry, and his private life suffered. In this book, Terry deals with his personal struggles and those of his team and the subsequent strains on his marriage.

I have admired Dave Diles' professionalism as a broadcaster and, in more recent years, as an author. Here he presents a straightforward, frank view of one of today's most publicized citizen-athletes and the trials and tribulations that accompany such fame.

When you have finished reading this book, I think you will agree with me that Terry Bradshaw is, and will continue to be, a positive force for us all, on and off the playing field.

—*Pete Rozelle*
Commissioner,
National Football League

Foreword

The man about whom this book is written is a good friend of mine. That he is a great quarterback is well-known. That's enough to make me admire him as an athlete, but my feeling for Terry Bradshaw goes much deeper than that because I know him as a fine Christian gentleman.

We've talked many times, very candidly, about the problems that we face as Christians and as professional football players. Like everyone in our business, Terry's had his ups and downs except that maybe his peaks have been higher and his valleys a little deeper. To me, he's always been a gregarious, open person.

We first met when he was coming into the National Football League in 1970. I had just finished my rookie season and we both attended a Fellowship of Christian Athletes get-together in Los Angeles. He and Mike Phipps were being honored that year. From the very first, he was an outgoing person and he seemed to have a lot of confidence. He didn't seem to be overwhelmed at being from a smaller college and being drafted number one in the country. That sort of thing could bowl some people over, but Terry seemed to be handling it very well. Not that he was cocky. It was just that he seemed to be carrying it all well. That impressed me, and one had to be impressed also by his physical appearance. I just knew down deep things weren't going to be easy for him and I was interested in watching how he developed and how he handled the problems that inevitably crop up.

I had been through the same thing the season prior to that and I just knew what was in store for someone in that situation. Coming into professional football as a rookie, I sort of felt I could do anything, you know. I could pass and I could run. I had been away from the game for four years (in naval service), but still it's a game. It was a physical thing and I had been successful at it, but I found out that it's a brand new kind of game. There's so much to learn and absorb and there's no way a person can do it in a hurry. It's much more than a physical game. It's sophisticated. It's played by people who are spending all their time at it. They know what they're doing, and experience is the main factor, especially for a quarterback. A running back can go about it a little differently because his main responsibility is to run with the football. It's vastly different when you're a quarterback. And a young quarterback can get hurt in a lot of ways, not just physically but psychologically. What's happened to a lot of these young quarterbacks who have come into the league is that they've wound up perhaps with the wrong teams, they've been faced with problems that can't be immediately solved, the teams and the public sometimes are not supportive, and some careers have been ruined.

There is no possible way a guy can come into this league as a rookie quarterback and set the world on fire, especially with a team that's not doing very well. It's too much of a load on the quarterback, and a rookie's just not equipped to handle that sort of pressure and responsibility. So I watched Terry very closely. He had a fine pre-season, but there was no way to turn that club around right away. I'm always concerned about young quarterbacks and worried that being thrown to the lions so quickly can destroy their confidence. That worried me with Terry, but looking back and knowing what he went through and how he suffered through some bad times to get where he is today makes me admire him all the more.

People think about the three Super Bowl victories he and the Steelers have had and they forget that he was knocked down to the point where they were going to trade him, he was so unhappy he felt he couldn't function any longer with the Pittsburgh team, and he came back. To me, that's the mark of a great athlete—the ability to bounce back from adversity. And that's the mark of a Christian, too.

All of us get knocked down. But it's the resiliency that really matters. All of us do well when things are going well, but the thing that distinguishes athletes is the ability to do well in times of great stress and urgency.

I remember playing the Steelers in Dallas in the final pre-season game in 1974 when Joe Gilliam was quarterbacking for them. He threw the ball all over the place and they nearly ran us out of the stadium. And it had been announced that Gilliam would be the club's starting quarterback that season. I talked with Terry after the game and he was really feeling in the pits. I tried to encourage him and told him to keep his chin up, and he said that things just looked very bad for him in Pittsburgh. That's a terrible thing to endure. Here he was, the man who was going to lead that club out of the wilderness, and now he was on the bench and figuring maybe he would be traded. But he bounced back, and that tells you a great deal about Terry Bradshaw the individual.

He was going through rough times in his personal life too, and the combination of those things is enough to defeat a lot of people or leave them permanently scarred. What some people don't seem to realize is that Christians are sinners too. They have problems like everyone else—sometimes more, it seems. People seem to think a Christian is perfect. He's not, but the important thing—the real difference—is that a Christian has Jesus Christ to come back to. A Christian has a home base, a place of refuge where he can gain strength. The Holy Spirit will still work in a Christian's life as long as he commits his life to the Lord, as long as he's trying. If we abandon Jesus Christ, we're in trouble. We may abandon the life style that Jesus expects us to have, but we can come back. That's the beautiful thing, and I know that's what happened to Terry. He just got off the path for a while, but the Lord came back in his life and handled not only the personal situation for Terry but the football situation as well. And I know Terry gives all the credit and glory to the Lord. He's kept his football in perspective with his total existence, and I believe that's what has helped him endure the problems he's had on the field and in his personal life. Without that inner strength, I really doubt whether Terry would ever have seen a Super Bowl.

Having been there, he's facing a whole new series of problems. He and I have talked about priorities in life. The Lord has to come first, our families second. And people do tug at us and try to pull us in different directions. We have a responsibility to our families to make money, and we have a greater responsibility to witness for the Lord. Sometimes we just have to say no to a lot of people and a lot of things, to give ourselves room to breathe. Everyone in the country wants Terry Bradshaw now. And he wants so much to please everyone. But he'll have to learn to say no to some people.

And there are problems unique to football. We may not like to face up to it, but we are in the entertainment business. We're in the limelight and the temptations are there. That's just the way our society is set up. But it goes back to basics and the commitments we make in life. We make a commitment as husband and wife and that should be enough; then we add to that the commitment we make to the Lord and then we're dealing with our permanent life, our salvation. That's how we overcome those temptations. There's a great bond between my wife and me, and we have an even greater bond with Jesus Christ. We're dealing with two worlds—the one we live in now and the one we want to live in eternally.

I'm not blind to some of the problems in football. There's every aspect of life in our game. Some former players have written about the game and have emphasized the negative side of it. It's a physical game, but it's not an overwhelmingly brutal game. I'm sure there's a drug situation, but I don't see it as an overpowering problem. We have to look at the big picture, and the big picture makes sense. It seems that some people just don't want to deal much with the positive side of it, yet the positive side definitely outweighs the negative.

Terry Bradshaw is a mighty positive force for professional

football and a powerful voice for the Lord. He's rugged and homespun and plain-talking and the type of athlete who makes the game worth playing, and the type of Christian I'm proud to have as a friend.

—*Roger Staubach*
Quarterback,
Dallas Cowboys

Terry Bradshaw:
MAN OF STEEL

Triumph and Turmoil

1 I've looked back on the whole thing a thousand times or more and I keep coming up with the same feelings. It was the best season of my life. But it was the worst too.

When you're the quarterback, it's wise to avoid superlatives. You should never think of something as the greatest, the best, the toughest, the unhappiest: you're playing a position that's tremendously inflated in its highs and lows and you're in a game where the outcome so often depends on emotion.

The late Vince Lombardi once said that professional football is 75 percent psychological. He was a lot smarter than I am—and if you believe what you read and hear these days, most everyone falls into that category—so I'll take his word for it. It's a tough, physical game—and yes, sometimes it's a very violent game—but it is emotional and psychological and mental as well.

If I live to be a hundred, I'll never understand how I kept myself in one piece emotionally during the 1978 pro football season. Everything seemed against it. We had been to the Super Bowl. We had won it twice. Maybe some folks thought we were fat and lazy, that we didn't care, that we lacked motivation and incentive, simply because it didn't mean so much to the Pittsburgh Steelers this time around. But from the day we checked into camp in the summer, it was obvious that the club was together, that the players had the right kind of determination and togetherness to do it again. No one said much about it, but in cases like this you don't have to say much. We're not a very demonstrative team anyway. We know what we are: we're tough and basically simple; we don't do much that's very complicated; we have good coaching and we're fundamentally sound; we play aggressively. A whole lot is said and written about character building, and people may think that's overrated. But I'm convinced that a team of good character—and by that I mean a bunch of guys who are morally sound and who really care about each other—will win the close games and come through in the clutch and perform well under adverse circumstances. Basically I think that's the makeup of our team.

As for myself, it's almost funny when people say I had the best season of my life and when I think of the flattering awards I've received. To me, the amazing thing is not that we put a good team on the field but that I was a part of it.

The truth is, I nearly went to pieces through the entire season. My marriage to Jo Jo Starbuck was just at the point where it should have been flowering. Instead we were struggling with our separate careers. We were apart most of the time. She was miserable. I was miserable. We were praying together each morning and each night over the telephone and reading favorite verses from the Bible to each other, trying to give each other strength and hope and inspiration. Instead, we were giving each other fits.

We were getting advice from everyone and ignoring most of it. Someone once said that marriages are made in heaven but we have to live them here on earth. And that's been our trouble. Much of the time, Jo Jo has been going her way and I have been going mine. There hasn't been much "our" way. Fortunately for both of us, we have managed to work together to try to figure out the answer to the most important question of all, What is *His* way?

Right now we are holding onto each other and to our Lord and trusting Him to solve the problems we cannot. We both know that through Him all things are possible. The real glory for Jo Jo's figure-skating career belongs to Jesus Christ, and whatever glory has come out of my football career belongs to Him, because God gave us our abilities and expects us to use them to the fullest.

Maybe that's why the Pittsburgh Steelers did so well last season. I'm not much for analyzing things and I didn't major in psychology. But maybe I was so consumed with my own personal problems that I didn't worry about football. And maybe I'm a better performer when I'm not worrying about football. I know I've always fretted a lot and concerned myself with whether everyone likes me. I've sought and needed approval from everyone. Perhaps that's a good amateur diagnosis, so I'll settle for that: I quit worrying about whether the coaches and the fans and the media liked Terry Bradshaw, because there were things far greater than football on my mind. And football will never rank higher than third in my personal ratings. My relationship with God comes first; my family comes next; and everything and everybody else finish in a dead heat for third as far as I'm concerned.

That's why, when it finally came time to get ready to play the Dallas Cowboys in the 1979 Super Bowl in Miami, I was able to stand up and meet the members of the press and say truthfully to them that getting to the Super Bowl was really more important than winning it. Some people misinterpreted what I said—I'm certain of that—but that's their problem and not mine. I said it and I meant it. Maybe I can embellish a little here and there and better explain my gut feeling going into Super Bowl XIII.

First, I had been there before and my teammates, for the most part, had been there before and we had experienced the joy of winning the Super Bowl. It's a one-shot deal, like a fight for the heavyweight championship of the world. Now this isn't to say that I didn't want to win it and wasn't prepared or able to put all I had into the preparation for winning it. It's just that I knew I wouldn't come unglued if we should lose. After all, the Cowboys are a fine team too, and Roger Staubach is a close friend of mine and a great Christian. Someone even made a not-too-funny joke about which team God might favor, since both Roger and I long ago had proclaimed our faith in Jesus

Christ. That's more odd than funny, because I'm certain God doesn't play favorites in athletic contests.

I thought mostly about winning and about game preparation. But down deep inside me I thought that if it happened that Dallas won the game, I'd be able to handle that kind of adversity. One of the great things I've learned since being a Christian is that just because we love God and believe in Him and trust in Him and have confidence that He will watch over us and someday take us to be with Him, it doesn't mean the life of a Christian will be easy. It seems to me the Bible is loaded with stories about great Christians who had tons of trouble and a lot of persecution and bad times. In fact, some of the greatest of Christians had the most trying times. I think God tests his people with adversity to see how they respond, and challenging that adversity can give us greater growth and strength in Him.

So I felt I was as prepared as I could possibly be for Super Bowl XIII. I felt good and I was physically prepared. I had studied all I could about the Cowboys and thought I understood their tendencies. I certainly had a good hold on our own personnel and what we thought we would be able to do in certain situations. And I was spiritually and emotionally prepared. Sure, winning is important and you should win every time if you can—it's important in a lot of ways to utilize your full potential and to give totally of yourself, and our guys were prepared for that—but in my own mind I was thankful to God for the achievements we had and for the chance to play in such an important game once more.

Sometime during the season, I guess I made peace with myself about my professional life and my personal life. It is tough and sometimes impossible for people to separate them. Because of the demands of my professional life and the demands Jo Jo has as a performer, our lives are intermingled and, you might say, in a confused state. But that feeling of peace carried right into the Super Bowl situation. I had to fight at times to keep that state of mind, but I know I kept it. When we went to Miami to get ready for the workouts, I knew from being there before that it would be bedlam. It's unreal, and unless a person has experienced it as a participant—and I mean by that, as a player and not a member of the media covering the game—I really don't think he can comprehend just what a mess it is.

I know it's necessary, all the hype and the other things that go with it, because it's a happening. So many millions of dollars are involved. Fortunately I went in pretty much prepared for that. I didn't figure to get any questions I hadn't heard before or couldn't handle. I knew I'd be asked about the quarterback match-up—the Naval Academy graduate and the kid from Louisiana Tech; the articulate and polished Dallas quarterback and the Li'l Abner from the bayous; the toothpaste smile and the one with tobacco juice dripping all over the place; and of course, the smart guy and the dummy. And I knew too just how I'd handle those things. I'm not as smart as Roger Staubach and not as smart as a whole lot of people, but I'm sick and tired of all that stuff about me being a dumb quarterback. I know how it all started. Trouble is, I don't know how to stop it.

I made up my mind I wouldn't worry about it, but at the same time, if that's all the folks from the press wanted to talk about, I'd just politely excuse myself. And when those things came up, that's just what I did. Matter of fact, I recall saying one time, "Gentlemen, if that's all you have on your mind, then I have better things to do." I wasn't trying to be a smart-aleck and I think I've always been cooperative with members of the press. Matter of fact, I love to talk, and I know the guys have to get a good story and I try always to give 'em one. But I'd simply had enough about my so-called stupidity.

The pitiful thing is, not a single reporter wanted to talk about my faith, my belief in God. One time when I brought it up during a news conference—and I do that often because it's important to me and it's just natural for it to pop up in my normal conversation—one reporter said to me, "We don't want to hear about that garbage, Terry." Isn't that a shame? It didn't make me mad, but I thought what a pathetic situation it is when people keep wanting to ask me questions about the Cowboys' famous Flex Defense, which I don't always totally understand, and don't want to hear a thing about the Creator of mankind. If that's a sign of the times, then we are living in bad times indeed. I never buttonhole others and try to force my beliefs on them, but Christianity is the single most important thing in my life. I felt that as one of the players on one of the competing teams, I might be able to witness for Jesus Christ. And I hoped that one writer or one broadcaster would choose to talk about that, rather than about the *x*'s and *o*'s of professional football.

But I never lost my cool and I don't think I made any enemies. Maybe I didn't convince anyone that I wasn't dumb, either, but I did my best. And that's the whole attitude, the entire atmosphere I had worked all season to create. I wanted to be in such a state of mind when I went there that I could keep from worrying about the winning or the losing of the football game. Some people got upset because I said early on that if I knew we were going to lose the Super Bowl, then I wouldn't even want to be there. After all, I had never experienced losing it, and naturally it crossed my mind that I might have to handle that sort of thing. Overall, though, I was able to keep things in perspective. I guess I merely isolated myself mentally, enjoyed myself, played, and had a good time. I had learned that I play better when I'm relaxed. Don't worry about the first two or three plays we plan to use, don't worry about the defense, don't worry about the crowd noise. Just relax. Do the job. Do it the best way you know how. I knew I had played well for several years and it was time for me to grow up and stop worrying.

I've always been the classic worrier. Am I doing a good job? Are the Rooneys proud of me? Am I earning too much money and not doing my job? Are the coaches happy with me? Are my teammates proud of me? Do they really think I can do the job? I always wanted everyone to like me. I wanted the city of Pittsburgh to be proud of me. Maybe this sort of behavior pattern was established in my childhood. But I grew up in a home where there was a lot of love and a willingness to express it openly to one another. I've always been accustomed to open, honest relationships where people don't hide their true feelings and where they reach out to each other.

Maybe some professional analyst will read this and say, "Hey, there's what's wrong with Bradshaw! He constantly needs approval." And I'll say, "Amen, I really do. I need it. I want it. I function better with it. And that's the way it is."

I knew that going into Super Bowl week would be chaotic. To top it off, my room was right by the swimming pool at our motel. And it was right next to a portable bar. So there was always the splashing of water: some had ice in it, some just people. There was a lot of noise at night, and I had trouble sleeping all week long. Plus there were planes flying over all the time. I thought some of them were close enough to strafe the motel. I didn't want to ask the club to change my room, because I didn't want to make waves. I never want to ask for special treatment. But it was a relief to get onto the field for our workouts. That was the only real escape, when we were actually on the field away from everyone else.

I didn't read any newspapers and I didn't watch any of the television newscasts. I developed a pattern years ago wherein I read the newspapers on Monday after the game, skip the weekdays when the press is building up the game, then start reading the sports pages again on Saturday to find out what certain high school teams are doing. By Saturday the writers have stopped writing the personal, so-called in-depth things. When you're building up for the Super Bowl, though, nothing escapes your attention. Certainly not the remark made by Thomas Henderson (Dallas linebacker, who said Terry couldn't spell CAT if you spotted him the C and the T) just a few days before the contest.

Henderson's remark didn't make me mad and it didn't hurt my feelings. I was humored by it because I tried to put myself in his shoes. I knew what he was trying to do. That's part of the psychology of the game. After all, he's a player and a very good one and he likes to be the center of attention. If I had thought Thomas Henderson really meant what he said, then I probably would have been upset. The press brought it to my attention and I gave my honest reaction. But they wouldn't let it die; they just kept harping on it. I guess they wanted a different reaction than the one I actually felt down deep inside, but I just couldn't create one for their benefit. So I finally lost my patience with the whole thing. Even those who defend me still use the word "dumb" and it's always there for the public to see. I'm not faulting anyone. I accept responsibility for the entire thing. Pat Haden is always going to be "too short to be a pro quarterback," and he's going to have to accept that. Terry Bradshaw is always going to be "too dumb to play quarterback in the National Football League" and I have to accept that. I'll continue to live with that, but I'm no fool. It'll be brought up until the day I retire and maybe until the day I die. It'll always be said of me that I was the guy who led his team to three Super Bowl championships—or maybe it'll be four or five by then—and who still found his intelligence questioned.

Some people who finally accepted me as a pretty decent quarterback almost apologize for it now. They say things like "Bradshaw finally figured out the game. He now can read defenses." I could do all those things four or five years ago. The ones who haven't yet accepted me can say, "Who couldn't throw with the receivers he has?" And you know, they're right. I accept that. I realize that. I have all the time in the world to throw the football. I have a great offensive line in front of me and great receivers to throw to. I'm on a great football team and I'm just one part of it and I realize that. And I realize that I was very fortunate in coming to a team when it had a 1-13 record, and I've been able to grow with that time. I'm a very lucky man and I know it. That's another reason I believe I was able to put Super Bowl XIII in perspective.

The day before the game we had our last workout. It was our first trip into the Orange Bowl, and we worked on our short-yardage and goal-line strategies and our kicking game. Then I came back to the hotel where my folks were staying, and we sat around and laughed and joked and played family card games all day. My mom and dad were there, my brothers Gary and Craig and their wives, Uncle Bobby and Aunt Margie who live on my ranch, my Uncle Duck and Aunt Betty from Bossier, my lawyer Gerald Burnett, and my accountant Gil Shanley—and of course Jo Jo, her mother, and her stepfather. There were lots of people around, family and friends. We didn't talk football. We played cards and talked about horses and cows and the ranch and all sorts of nice things. I guess we sat around for about eight hours, from two in the afternoon until ten at night. I had to be in at eleven.

All season long I had trouble sleeping because Jo Jo was away and I'd wake up during the night. But since she was with me in Miami, I got a good night's sleep. It was six in the morning when I woke up, and the first thing I did was to look out the window to check on the weather. It was raining so hard I could barely see the parking lot. It was coming down in buckets and I was happy as a pig in slop. After all, we're the foul-weather team. Then I thought, "Oh no, they'll have the field covered." Still, I thought it wouldn't be so bad for us if it rained all during the game.

Jo Jo was still sleeping, and I knelt down and prayed. I remember that I thanked God for once again giving us the opportunity to play in the Super Bowl, and I asked that every man on both teams appreciate the skills the Good Lord gave us in order for us to get that far. I asked that the Lord relax the players and relieve them of all pressures so they could perform to the best of those abilities. I asked for strength and confidence and that no one be hurt. I had some special people on my prayer list and I prayed for them, for the leaders of the world, and for my family.

I got dressed, kissed Jo Jo, and went down to have some coffee. It was only 6:30 A.M. when I came into the Steelers' reception room. A few people were there setting up tables and I started drinking coffee. I was itchy—I couldn't wait to get to the ballpark. But our pre-game get-together wasn't scheduled until eleven because the game was a late-afternoon starter. So I went back to the room, talked with Jo Jo for a while, then went back to the reception room. Nothing I did would make the time go faster. I drank lots of coffee. I didn't eat a bite: I never eat before a game. Nothing. Finally we had our pre-game meal and I sipped on some coffee. Then we had a thirty-minute quarterback meeting with the coach and I caught the first bus for the stadium.

Our coach, Chuck Noll, may be tense and all that, but he didn't show it. Maybe that's why he's such a great coach. He knew we were all wound up tight and he tried to relax us. He was smiling. We went over what we call the Dallas "tendencies," what the Cowboys are likely to do in certain situations, how we're going to try to counteract those tendencies, what we'll try to do in certain situations. We went over the first three plays we planned to use and he said, "Okay, let's go out and have fun. Let the good times roll. Just relax and enjoy this. It's what we've been working for all year long."

And that's what we did. I think we were pretty relaxed, considering the two-week buildup all of us had endured. We didn't boggle our minds with the technicalities of the Dallas system. It is a complicated system, and it's been called a Computer Offense and a Flex Defense and all that, but it's effective because the Cowboys have talented, mobile people on their team. No one had to juice me up to have respect for the Dallas Cowboys. No one had to remind me, either, that I'd never really played very well against them. We'd won some games, but I personally had never played that well.

I don't remember much at all about the bus ride to the stadium. I recall that when we got there, we had to go all the way around the stadium and then we were stopped because the Dallas Cowboys' cheerleaders had a police escort that was blocking our way. They let the cheerleaders through first.

As for the pre-game activity in the locker room, I honestly don't think it was any different from that of a regular game. I chewed a lot of bubble gum and got dressed early. I couldn't wait to get onto the field, but the game was still three hours away when we got there. I just walked around, listened to some music, watched some of the guys playing backgammon, and stood around while some of the others got taped up. I felt great physically, but I kept watching the clock.

When we finally went out onto the field for the pre-game warmup is when I really felt the butterflies. It wasn't like the first trip to the Super Bowl, because then I remember the crowd noise just scared the daylights out of me and that's all I could think about. This time I felt good the minute I got onto the field. I went over and talked to Roger and said a word or two to Cliff Harris and Charlie Waters (Dallas defensive backs) and two coaches of theirs—Gene Stallings, who used to be at Texas A & M, and Ernie Stautner, the old Steeler great. I talked to a whole bunch of the Cowboys before I ever picked up a football. I was just feeling my way around, I guess. Then I went over and started warming up.

Once the game started, I really was feeling good about our chances. After all, we were an experienced team. We had been there before. We knew what we could do. We knew we were playing a tremendous opponent. All I wanted to do was to help us play our game and let things take care of themselves. I vividly remember the third play of the game. We needed a chunk of yardage and we wanted to see how the Cowboys were gonna play our tight end, Randy Grossman. We felt they would double-team our wide receivers, and so we called an "individual" to Grossman with blitz control in case they safety-blitzed. It was close, but Randy had good concentration and caught the ball with Waters covering him man-for-man and we got the first down.

Football games have many turning points and lots of key plays, and the first one in Super Bowl XIII was when the Cowboys were driving and turned over the ball. They might have gotten seven points, or at least three, but instead we got the ball and got a little drive of our own going. (*The Steelers went 53 yards in 7 plays after the Cowboys had driven 51 yards only to lose the ball on Drew Pearson's fumble of a Tony Dorsett pitch at the Pittsburgh 47-yard-line.*)

We took it right in, but my pass to John Stallworth was not what you'd call a thing of beauty. It was an end-over-end job, the ugliest thing you can imagine, and John made a great catch. There were two key plays before that—the hook pass on third and long to Grossman, and the one to Stallworth when the Cowboys blitzed me and I unloaded the ball. Then I went play-action again and hit Stallworth and he made a one-handed grab out of bounds. Then I came right back with another play-action pass and hit Stallworth on a flag in the corner of the end zone. He leaped up and caught the ball and dragged his left foot in. It was an unbelievable catch. Now we're seven points up when we could have been trailing. But as I said, the touchdown pass was horrible. I was shocked that somebody didn't shoot that thing in the air: it was like a wounded duck.

The Cowboys showed their character when they went right back up the field and scored to tie the game. Then I fumbled—or they stole the ball, whatever you want to call it—and they scored again. I was actually laughing to myself coming off the field after the turnover, and people who saw me must have thought I was out of my mind. But you have to admit, it was funny. And besides, I guess I wanted everyone to know that everything was fine. I guess I was saying to the whole world, "Look, folks. See, it's not bothering me. Don't y'all worry 'bout it, 'cause everything's gonna be all right." And I really felt that way. I felt like "Hey, they scored! So what? So we're down 14-7. So what? We'll just come back and score again." Maybe I had no business feeling that way, but I did. And I was injured too, but it was nothing serious and I knew I'd be back.

Now, you talk about luck! The play we scored on next to tie the game again was a piece of work! A 6-yard pass and a 69-yard run—and it goes into the books as a 75-yard touchdown pass. It was a simple hook to Stallworth: he takes it and Aaron Kyle makes a stab at him and misses and he picks up a block from Lynn Swann and goes in for a touchdown. Dallas tries to get something going again, but Mel Blount intercepts one of Roger's play-action passes with less than two minutes to play in the second quarter. Talk about the momentum switching back and forth! Migosh, here they might have gone in to take the lead at the half and instead we get the ball back and we go into our two-minute drill. Everyone remembers that the big play in this was the controversial pass to Swann in which I unloaded the ball with a blitz coming and Swann went after it along with one of their guys. I've seen the play on film dozens of times since, and I still can't make up my mind about the official's interference call. All I know is their feet got tangled up, the call went our way, and I'm delighted that it did. It set us up in good field position at their thirty. Lots of people keep screaming about that call, but they forget that we didn't score on that play. The Cowboys still could have stopped us—but they didn't.

When we were finally set up to a point where we thought we could get seven or at least three, I called the option pass that got us our third touchdown. Now, it wasn't very pretty, either, I'll admit. We had shown the play during the season, where both wide receivers come inside on double slants: the back goes out to the flat; when I come outside, if their guys stay outside, then I hit Rocky Bleier right now for a touchdown. But Dallas zoned off instead of playing man-for-man. They merely dropped off. I came inside, and both my inside guys were covered, so I had to move out of the way of some pressure and got outside. Swann and Stallworth went inside and they were covered. Rocky was in the middle in a crowd and I was sitting there with the ball. The Cowboys were looking at me and I was looking at them. I think one of their linebackers, D. D. Lewis, had Rocky covered and I felt enough pressure to know I had to do something fast. So I arched the ball back to the middle. I just put a little touch pass on it and Rocky, who's only five-ten went way up and outjumped everyone for the ball. He actually stopped and arched way back and caught the ball behind Lewis for the touchdown. Now, I can't even put that feeling into words. It was just beautiful! It gave all of us a great lift. We were holding onto a 21-14 lead at the half.

The halftime thing in the locker room was pretty routine actually. We had our group meetings, the coaches went over the tendency charts, and then we shared some thoughts and we were ready to go back out there. We took our normal time, did what we normally do, and couldn't wait to get back out there and finish the job. But we had to wait: the halftime show wasn't nearly over. We had to wait an extra ten minutes. I don't know what that long wait did to the Cowboys, but I know it flattened out our entire team. At least I was flat.

Back on the field again, it seems like a different ball game. Different atmosphere, different everything. We had begun in daylight and now it's just about dark. It's colder and damper. The field is a little dewy. And I go out there and call a terribly conservative game. I'm hoping we can run the football and eat up the clock and sit on a seven-point lead and wait for a break and then capitalize on it. I'm suddenly playing the game I didn't want to play at all.

Maybe it was then that I finally realized what an important game this was. This was no World Series where we have as many as seven games to determine the champion. We had just one game, but the way I started the second half it was as if I were trying to make two separate football games out of it.

Instead of playing to win, I am playing not to lose. And they're kicking us. They drive down and kick a field goal. We get the ball back and one, two, three and we're out. Our defense is on the field for practically the whole third quarter. Finally we wake up, and I start doing the things that got us here in the first place. We start a pretty good drive and then I get a delay-of-game penalty on third down.

That's when Thomas Henderson caught me and spun me around and eased me to the ground. Franco Harris got mad. He thought Thomas should have heard the whistle and stopped, but it was no big deal.

Anyway, we have to back up five more yards. I figure down in there, the Cowboys will blitz. They know I'm gonna pass. So I call a trap, anticipating blitz, and Franco goes all the way through the middle. There again, it's the emotional part of the game. Franco really wanted the football, and when a man really wants it, he can do much better things with it.

We get the ball back on the kickoff when we recover a fumble, and I call the same pass to Swann that I called to Stallworth for the first touchdown. Lynn is supposed to go out to the flag. He sees the cornerman outside, sees the safety come up, and knows he can play the outside very easily. Swann sees it, I see it, so he stays inside and behind Cliff Harris and I fire the ball and he makes a great catch. Touchdown! We're up by 18 points.

Two things happened that got me a trifle upset on the bench. I guess the public address announcer told the fans I had set a passing record and someone, I don't remember who, came over and told me. Records don't mean anything, particularly at a time like that. Then once we got that 18-point lead, some of our guys started celebrating. I told 'em to hush up, that we really didn't have anything to celebrate just yet and we should save our party till later. My insides told me that we had the thing won, but I knew we couldn't afford to get careless and make mistakes, not against a team like Dallas. Yeah, I was on some of them a little bit, but I was actually getting on myself, too, because of my own feeling that we had done it, we had won—we had won our third Super Bowl. Believe me, though, our guys got a lot quieter when the Cowboys came down and scored two more touchdowns. The final score was 35–31.

It was bedlam after the game. I know that Roger and I met on the field and shook hands. I don't remember what was said, but he's such a classy human being I know he made me feel terrific. Over the roar of the crowd and all the confusion in trying to get to the locker room to celebrate with my teammates, I said a quiet little prayer of thanks to God for doing so much for a kid from Louisiana. I couldn't think of a thing I had done to deserve all this.

Months later, I still can't. But I'm very thankful.

For the record, Terry Bradshaw was the unanimous choice as the most valuable player in Super Bowl XIII. He set game records of 318 yards passing and 4 touchdown passes, both career highs for him. He completed 17 of 30 passes, hitting Stallworth on a 28-yarder for the first score; hooking up with Stallworth on a 75-yarder for the second; connecting with Bleier from the 7-yard-line; and capping off the day with the 18-yarder to Swann.

During the regular season, Bradshaw won the American Football Conference passing title with an 84.8 rating and led the league in touchdown passes with 28 (36 including postseason games) and that's the highest total since the professional football merger of 1970. For the second year in a row, his teammates elected him the club's most valuable player. It is worth noting that in three Super Bowl appearances, Bradshaw has completed more than 55 percent of his passes, thrown for 7 touchdowns, and suffered but 1 interception.

Along for the Ride

2 I never really felt I was much a part of the other Super Bowl victories. I wasn't supposed to be.

It wasn't a matter of Terry Bradshaw leading anyone to victory or being expected to accomplish anything bordering on the spectacular. It was strictly a case of the Steelers having an outstanding team and if Bradshaw doesn't foul up, then they might come out on top. Don't mess up, Brad, and we can be right in there. Don't make any stupid mistakes, Terry, and we might pull it off. Just hand off to your running backs, try not to fumble the ball, and don't throw it up for grabs. Be conservative. Be careful. In other words, I was just along for the ride. Someone had to be in there in the huddle and take the snap from the center, and I felt I was elected for that job almost by default.

Coach Chuck Noll had three quarterbacks in the 1974 season. I had done most of the starting the previous season—I missed four games because of a separated shoulder—and I left for my ranch that winter assuming that I'd be the starting quarterback. When it came time for camp to open the next summer, there were Terry Hanratty, Joe Gilliam, and me. Trouble was, Hanratty and Bradshaw *weren't* there because of the players' strike. I finally went in ahead of some of the others and maybe that ticked off some players. I had given it a lot of

35

prayerful consideration and I felt I had made my point by staying out and sticking with the players' association, but it then came time for me to be about the business of making a living and getting to work. By the time I got to camp, though, the coach had apparently made up his mind to go with Joe Gilliam.

For the first time in my life, I felt like walking away from the game that had meant so much to me. I mean, from the time I was a scrawny kid I had eaten and slept football, and I had that boyhood dream to someday be a quarterback in the National Football League. And now all that was being taken away from me. That was but the final blow in a series of setbacks that left me wondering about myself as a man, as an athlete, but most importantly as a Christian. I had to make a settlement with my God before I could accomplish anything else. And I had to admit that I was a phony. I was acting the part of a Christian and not living it. It was a sore that had been festering for four years.

My first season with the Steelers was much more than I expected, even though I had been the first player drafted. After all, no one expects to jump out of college—especially from a little school like Louisiana Tech—and into a starting quarterback's job in the National Football League. Here again, maybe it happened by default because the Steelers had done so poorly for so many seasons. But I started 8 of our 14 regular season games. I even threw 6 touchdown passes. It's only fair to point out that I also threw 24 interceptions: the touchdown passes weren't a league record, but the interceptions were. Even though I had brashly promised the fans of Pittsburgh a Super Bowl, I was smart enough to realize just how young and inexperienced I was and how much I had to learn. And I was smart enough not to have promised them a Super Bowl right away.

My second year I started all but one game, and the club had its best record in eight years (6 wins, 8 losses). Then we got Franco Harris the following season and won 11 games against only 3 losses and got into the playoffs. Outwardly it was everything a young man could hope for. I had dated a girl through my first two seasons, then married this former Miss

Teenage America in February of 1972. By the following season, everything was going south. My shoulder got banged up and so did my marriage. I threw 7 interceptions in the first two games after getting back into the lineup, then threw 3 more in a wild playoff game we lost to the Oakland Raiders. I was just as erratic off the field. The truth of the matter is, I had separated myself from God. I lived only for Terry Bradshaw, not for God. I tried to be one of the boys and went to every honky-tonk I could find and chased women and behaved in a way that was totally alien to anything I had ever known before. I—the big I—was in control of my life, and frankly, my whole life was out of control.

The problems in camp prior to the '74 season finally tipped my cart right over. I was wallowing in self-pity. All I did was mope around and feel sorry for myself. Someone would write something unflattering about me in the newspapers and I'd be mad at him. Someone would make an unkind remark on television and I'd flare up again. "Terry's a dumb quarterback! . . . The Steelers made a bad investment! . . . He'll never make it in the pros! . . . He throws too many interceptions! . . . Li'l Abner! . . . Ozark Ike!" I just figured the whole world was down on me and the Pittsburgh fans were leading the jeers. I had no really close friends. I had no spiritual counselor. I wasn't bothering to attend church. I rarely prayed. And I knew the guys on the club figured I was the biggest hypocrite in the world. I didn't know whether the coach hated me or just chose to ignore me. I was sure he didn't like me. In fact, I had so doggoned much sympathy for myself I didn't figure anybody liked me. Then it occurred to me that I wasn't very likable: I didn't like me myself! And how could I? I wasn't even being myself. I was trying to be someone else and was doing a rotten job of it.

For the first six games of the 1974 season I sat on the bench. Much of that time I pouted and sulked and grumbled to myself. I felt like a leper. I wasn't even a part of the team.

One day in early October I came home from practice and sat down in a big chair in my apartment and took a little self-inventory. Some years later I saw a little sign that read, "When there's no way out, there's a way UP," and I wish I could say that I saw that sign back then and it triggered some mechanism in me that woke me up and got me on the right track. But there were no signs, no messages, no flashes of light, and no bolts of lightning. I wasn't struck blind as Saul of Tarsus was. I just put my head in my hands and began to cry and tremble all over and finally I blurted out, "Here I am, God. I've tried to handle it all by myself and I just can't get the job done. So I'm placing my life in Your hands. I need some peace of mind and I know You can give it to me. From this minute on, You're the boss. You're number one." Then I prayed for a long time, and I remember it as if it were last night. I really felt as if someone had lifted a piano off my shoulders. I felt stronger mentally and physically. I knew I couldn't do anything about what had happened in the past, but I was aware that with God's help I could do a whole lot about everything that happened from that minute forward. And I made up my mind that Terry Bradshaw was going to be a real, sincere, honest, and up-front human being and take whatever lumps life had to give him—and on top of that, I'd not complain about the bad times and I'd give God the credit and glory when the times were good. And somehow I knew they'd be good again. Being a starting quarterback didn't matter. Getting to the Super Bowl didn't matter. What mattered was that I was myself again and I was determined to stay that way.

A week or so later, I was the starting quarterback again. Then a couple of weeks after that, I wasn't the starting quarterback again. But this time I had a good attitude about it. I think back to all the faces I put on for the press and the public and it's ridiculous really. When I came up to Pittsburgh from Louisiana I was a hick—and I guess I still am—but I've always loved to talk, so I talked. The Steelers hadn't ever won anything so I told 'em we'd win. That's what they wanted to hear, wasn't it? I couldn't say we were gonna keep losing. How would that have sounded? It was very hard for me to relax, because I wanted to prove so badly to the public, to the other players—hey! to myself—that I belong here in Pittsburgh. You know, I'm gonna make it. I'm gonna be good. We're gonna win. I didn't believe it myself, but I figured if I kept repeating it maybe I'd come to believe it. And I was shy, introverted. The other players treated me well, but there was no real warmth and fellowship, probably because I left the definite impression that I didn't want it that way. I wouldn't let people like me or get close to me. I was a loner and that was it. Off the field, I rarely had anything to do with any of the other players. I kept to myself. When I tried to make conversation or tell a little story I thought was funny, I got trampled in the conversation. I'd be sitting there trying to get the words out and wham!—the whole thing would go right past me. I was baffled by it all. And the less I contributed, I guess the dumber some people thought I was. So most of the time I just didn't have anything to say.

When I got the starting job back, I didn't set the woods on fire. Someone pointed out to me later that I had only 8 interceptions for the whole 1974 season but they must have forgotten that it's tough to get intercepted when you're sitting on the bench. We beat Buffalo and Oakland to earn the right to play in the Super Bowl. Even though it was Pittsburgh's first division championship in forty-two years, the whole affair had a hollow ring to it. I was delirious with joy for the club, but in no way did I feel I had been a major factor in getting there. I guess I agreed with one of the writers who said words to the effect that a tackling dummy playing quarterback could have gotten the job done with the running attack and the defense we had.

That was the prevailing atmosphere when we went to New Orleans to get ready to play the Minnesota Vikings in Super Bowl IX. In all the pre-game buildup, my role was secondary. Oh, I was interviewed and asked a lot of questions—well, not a lot of different questions, but a lot of people asked me pretty much the same line of questions. It was all centered around my ability, or lack of ability, as a quarterback. Did I have confidence? Could I get the job done? Fran Tarkenton was smart and Terry Bradshaw was dumb. It was basically a simple script: The Steelers had a tough defense and good runners and "Terry, do you think you'll foul things up?" I tried to be cooperative, but when I went back to my room each night, I prayed just for strength to endure each day. I guess I was a lot like an alcoholic, simply praying to get through one day at a time. I knew when I got up each morning

I'd have to face the same thing all over again. And there's no question that I was very, very jittery when we went into Tulane Stadium on January 12, 1975, to play the game at last.

Sure, I had rededicated myself to Jesus Christ. I knew my personal life was unfulfilled because I was lonely, and each night I prayed for God to send me a Christian woman to love. But I knew everything was in good shape and in His hands and that whatever happened, in football or in any other part of my life, I could accept it. I knew I could accept victory and not be overwhelmed by it and I knew I could accept defeat as a challenge from God. Finally I was beginning to learn the true meaning of the words "Not my will, but Thine." Despite the fact that I had grown up in a Christian environment with lots of good Christian love and despite the fact that I was in the house of the Lord in those early years, I still was a baby Christian. I was just beginning to learn about God. The God I knew as a child scared me and I was always afraid of doing something wrong. I kept thinking of Him as a punishing God who was gonna get me if I did something wrong. Now I was being introduced to the loving and caring and merciful God, the God who never wants to see one of His children hurt in any way. To get to know that God, I had to turn over my life to Him, to be really submissive and obedient no matter what. When I got to that point, I began to develop poise, confidence, maturity. I began to understand that as I grew as a Christian, I grew in every other way as well.

Our team chaplain had done wonders with me and had opened up a whole new avenue for understanding my own faith and God's love for me. He thought after we beat the Buffalo Bills in our first playoff game that I might make a public announcement about the direction my life was taking. It's not that he was pushing me to do it; I think we both knew it would happen; it was just a question of when. I guess he thought I'd do it after we beat the Raiders. Believe me, I prayed plenty about it, and the time didn't seem right. Maybe it was the ham in me. Maybe I was unconsciously waiting for the big audience.

My performance against the Minnesota Vikings in Super Bowl IX was not very artistic. The first time we had the ball I tried to pass on third down and got dumped for a loss. Then I had a completion in the flat, got thrown for another loss, missed a receiver, and a few plays later overthrew Frank Lewis. Even with my slopping things up the way I did, we had two chances to score in the first period, but Roy Gerela missed one field goal try and the next time we got a bad snap and never got the kick off. I wasn't any more impressive in the second period. I think I tried only three or four passes and they didn't remind anyone of Sammy Baugh. *(Terry actually threw five: the Steelers were penalized for interference on one, two others gained 27 yards, and another lost 6 yards.)* But as everyone predicted at the outset, our defense gave us good field position and we got a safety and managed to hold onto a 2-0 lead at the half.

In the third period—that defense again. We got a break on the kickoff when Minnesota fumbled and we recovered at their 30-yard-line. We ran at 'em four times and I gave it to Franco Harris the last three in a row and we bounced in to score. The Vikings made it 9-6 early in the fourth quarter when they recovered a blocked punt in the end zone, but we came right back with a long drive and got the score right back. *(The drive was 66 yards, and Terry passed successfully three times in three attempts for a total of 40 yards including a 4-yard scoring strike to Larry Brown. For the game, Bradshaw was 9 of 14 in passing for 96 yards and ran the ball 5 times for 33 yards.)*

Some people may choose not to believe it, but I really never got a great charge out of winning the Super Bowl. I enjoyed it and I wanted to win, but it didn't give me a great personal lift. I didn't feel vindicated or anything else, because I had confidence in myself and my own destiny and I wasn't really concerned over what was written or said about me. All that mattered was what God thinks of me. But I had made a promise to God. He never once let me down, and I knew this would be one tremendous opportunity to confess my faith in God publicly. He has commanded us to do that, you know. I was so glad that God loves me and that I love Him that I felt obligated to say it where I could reach the most people. And that's why, when I was surrounded by the media people in the locker room after the game, I told of the turnaround in my life, my faith in Jesus Christ, and my commitment to God.

I was starting to fit in with the team. I've never been what you'd call a joiner, but the pieces started fitting together and the players started being more friendly with me and making me a part of the locker-room jokes. Maybe it's because I opened up more and was more outgoing to them. It wasn't that I had thought a lot of players disliked me; I guess I had thought maybe they just didn't care one way or the other. Through the confidence I was developing and a little taste of success, I started being myself and quit worrying so much. Football is something you have to prove out on the field, and if things are going well there, it makes for happier times off it.

As we started the 1975 season, all of us were pretty confident about our team overall. Nobody was comparing me with any of the fine quarterbacks around, and I neither expected it nor deserved it. But I was at the place where I felt I could contribute something once in a while instead of being just a robot. Someone told me once that '75 was almost like two different seasons for me. (*Terry completed 62 percent of his passes through the first ten games and only 45 percent in the last four. He set a team record for accuracy and had the best touchdown-interception ratio of his career, 18 touchdowns and only 9 interceptions.*) But mainly I was learning not to run with the football. Till then I knew I could take a good lick, and I enjoyed running the ball and maybe I was too quick to toss aside the possibilities of a pass and take off running. The experts have a way of describing that: they say when a quarterback takes off running, it means either he's scared to stay in the pocket and get hit or else he's not sharp enough to locate a secondary receiver. Whatever the case, I ran less and less and mostly out of panic or necessity. I still hadn't won over the Pittsburgh fans, and for me to say that I didn't realize it or didn't hear the catcalls when I fouled up would be a lie. Even when we earned the right to play in the Super Bowl for the second year in a row, it was another of those don't-mess-it-up-Terry situations. I don't say that out of sympathy for myself—God knows I had enough of that and I had worked my way out of that rut—but that's simply the way it was. We ran the ball down the Cowboys' throats. We passed when we had to. We played mean, stout defense. And that's how we won the Super Bowl again. We pretty much controlled their running game, and we intercepted three of Staubach's passes. Our guys sacked Roger seven times.

From the fans' standpoint, the game was pretty dull until the final fifteen minutes. We were losing 10-7 when Reggie Harrison blocked Mitch Hoopes' punt and we got a safety when the ball rolled through the end zone. We got the ball back and moved down—staying on the ground every play—close enough for Gerela to kick a field goal to put us ahead 12-10 about halfway through the period. Then we got another big break when Mike Wagner intercepted Roger's pass on the first play after the kickoff and took it down to the Cowboys' seven-yard-line. We had to settle for another field goal and were ahead by five points. Talk about defense! Right up to that time, our guys had let the Cowboys have only seven plays in three possessions when we got the ball at our own thirty with about 4½ minutes to play. We got the break we had been looking for. Lynn Swann got loose on a third-and-four situation and I hit him at the five-yard-line and he skipped in for the touchdown that put us ahead 21-10. We held on to win 21-17. Funny, I don't remember much about the ending of that game. I got banged pretty solidly on the touchdown pass to Swann and was woozy for a long time.

It was a great victory for our team. Just think—two straight Super Bowls after never having won anything in all those years of trying. As for me, I finally knew I was Chuck Noll's quarterback no matter what, and even if the Pittsburgh fans didn't love me, I could once again like myself and I knew God loved me and that would have been enough, even without that second Super Bowl ring.

(Terry Bradshaw now has three Super Bowl rings to his credit and wears none of them. His father, Bill Bradshaw, wears the one from Super Bowl IX which Terry gave to him as a gift. Terry gave the ring from Super Bowl X to his older brother Gary.)

If there were a contest to elect the most popular owner in the National Football League, Art Rooney of the Pittsburgh Steelers would win in a unanimous voice vote. It is no secret that for years, insiders around the league rooted for the Steelers out of great affection for their owner. On provocative issues laid before the lords of professional football, Art Rooney wanted only to know what was right.

Well into his seventies before his team ever won as much as a divisional championship, Art Rooney has celebrated only modestly his team's recent accomplishments, winning three Super Bowl confrontations. Around the league there is great jubilation for him. To say that he is one of the nice human beings in the game is to suggest tacitly that other owners are not so nice. So be it. He does not need the ownership of the club either for self-gratification nor as a tax shelter. He owns the Steelers because he loves them. He is in his office each morning but only after attending church services. He has the same friends he did years ago, and while he is uncommonly successful and uncommonly influential, he is truly a common man. He is as much at home—perhaps more—with scruffy old codgers down on their luck and looking for a fast twenty as he is with giants of the political world and titans of industry. And players who suggest that the professional game is a dehumanizing thing never met Art Rooney. His love for his players is a very real thing, and he particularly loves Terry Bradshaw:

"You know, the Steelers had a history of bad first draft choices. We'd either draft wrong or something. Anyway, we wound up discarding them, the way we did Johnny Unitas. We've missed so many good players over the years. We agreed that Terry was going to be our number one draft choice and we made up our minds that we were going to go with him. He was going to be our quarterback. We got tremendous offers to trade Terry, but we weren't tempted.

"We got him on a coin flip. The Chicago Bears had tied us as the worst team in professional football. We won the toss and took Terry. My son Artie, who's in charge of our draft, followed Terry's college career and we felt he had everything: size, ability, the arm, durability—everything. It took time, but it all finally came together.

"In the early years, there were difficult times. I'd kid Terry a lot and sit with him on the team bus. So often he'd be sitting by himself. He seemed to be down. I didn't give him much advice—I try to stay out of people's way—but I remember telling him to have patience and things would work out. It's awfully tough for a young person to have patience. I guess you acquire patience when you get older.

"I remember during one period of time—he was single and he's a very handsome man and an athlete and all that—there'd be a young lady or so waiting at the airport to see him. Once we landed and there was this lady waiting and she came right up and hugged and kissed him. Maybe the next day I remarked to him that of all the ladies I'd seen around him, that one was the nicest filly I'd seen. Then he told me it was his mother.

"There were times when I knew he was losing confidence and I suppose I'd purposely seek him out. He was going through a tough time, and I was so certain he'd be a magnificent quarterback. I never second-guessed the coach on what he was doing with the quarterback situation, even when the boys were being shuffled around a little bit. I think when you hire a coach you let him do the job. I'm sure he knows more about football than I do, and he surely knows more about the players. In all the years here, I've never interfered and I never allow anyone who works for me to second-guess the coach, even though it's the easiest thing in the world to do.

"But in the last few seasons, you could just see this greatness coming together. It was like the realization of a dream. The talent was there all along: it's a God-given thing. And I was rooting so hard for it to happen for Terry because he's very outward, very honest. There's nothing phony about Terry. You just have to like him, just have to know what a great person he is. Everyone in our organization thinks very highly of him as a human being. I simply don't know how you can fault him. He's the ideal man.

"Now, when we won the first Super Bowl, I guess that was the happiest time of all for me because we hadn't won at all, and after you don't win for so long, people think you don't know what it's all about. They think you weren't trying. But I think you try harder when you're losing. You give it more time because you're worrying and trying to figure out all the things you're doing wrong. I wasn't at all sure we'd win the first Super Bowl we were in. I was confident we'd win the next one, and this last one—well, I was absolutely sure we'd win it. No doubt in my mind. This was Terry's team. When he first came here, some folks said he wasn't the Pittsburgh type because he was from another part of the country and he spoke in a little different way. But he's Pittsburgh all the way. He's tough and durable. Nothing fancy. Nothing put on. Just right out in the open. And he plays hurt.

"I've been around horses all my life and we talk about great horses having heart. They don't want to get beat. They almost refuse to get beat. They know where that winner's circle is and they want to get there. They simply have a lot of courage, or heart. And Terry's like that. Heart is what often separates a good horse from a great horse and a good athlete from a great one. And with our ball club, I really think we have a close-knit family. When we were at the other park, we dressed in a house, down in the cellar. How the players ever got in and out of there I'll never know. We just weren't first class. When we moved into Three Rivers Stadium, it brought all of us closer. Our offices are here. We practice here. We play our games here, and we see a lot more of the ball players. We communicate with each other and get to know each other. If there's a secret, I think that's it. Maybe some owners don't want to get too close to their players, but I don't think you can be too close. It's better if they know you care about them. And when you have a quarterback like Terry, who's such a moral person—well, everybody just sort of looks up to him. He's a fellow you can believe in."

The Monkey on My Back

There is nothing so believable as an oft-repeated lie.

—Anonymous

A lie has no legs, and cannot stand; but it has wings, and can fly far and wide.

—Warburton

3 I never told anyone in the world I was smart. But I'm not dumb, either. Yet for as long as I live and for as long as people talk about football and the people who played it, I'll be remembered as the guy who got to a few Super Bowls even though he wasn't what you'd call brilliant.

I've described myself as a baby Christian because there's so much I have to learn, so many things I have not yet discovered. Sometimes I marvel at the things others know about the Bible and about God and the great history in His Word. For many years it didn't occur to me how even to approach His Word, and I had no real idea how to study the Bible, nor how to search for answers. But since I started getting better about my Bible study work and made a new commitment to a meaningful, daily relationship with the Lord, I've been amazed at the things I have learned and the answers I have found in the Scriptures.

When I went through my divorce, I found comfort in the

Bible that I couldn't find anywhere else in the world. During all the time the fans in Pittsburgh were on my back and even cheering when I got hurt, I turned to the Bible and found understanding there that helped me through that long crisis. It's a strength that man cannot provide, no matter how strong he may be and no matter how tough his will. Sitting around in an apartment, knowing you've lost your job, knowing the fans don't like you, figuring your coach has given up on you, knowing you've failed to make a go of a marriage, being separated from the only people you know really care about you, reading in the papers and hearing on television that you're a dumb hick—well, it can drive you a little crazy unless there's something else in your life that's more important than all these other things put together. I moped around that little apartment in Pittsburgh, played and sang every sad country song coming and going, chewed tobacco and spit juice until that coffee can was almost overflowing, and wondered if I'd ever amount to a hill of beans—until I found peace with God. Once that happened, I was ready to face myself for what I really was and then I was prepared to face the world.

Now don't get me wrong. Don't think I'm equating myself with the martyrs of biblical days. But all of us think we're persecuted at some stage of our lives. And I've never met a person who likes criticism. If you enjoy criticism, then perhaps you're demented. But when I felt I was being attacked from all sides, man, I found a whole lot of people in the Bible—and I mean super Christians who built the early church—who had tons of trouble and who really went the distance for their beliefs. They were stoned, put in prison, tortured, killed—you name it. And they stood up to it. I found some wonderful passages in the Bible that gave me strength during those bad times. I've obtained some Bible study aids over the years and they help me look for specific things for particular needs, even particular moods. All through the Psalms, David cried out to the Lord and talked about how many people had risen up against him (Psalm 3) and asked for deliverance from those who persecuted him (Psalm 7). And sometimes he felt God wasn't listening to him (Psalms 10 and 13) and he felt terribly alone and misunderstood. Probably the most comforting words for me come from the Gospel of Matthew, especially the Sermon on the Mount. Jesus talked about how the saved are really blessed when people persecute them, and how a Christian has to expect that sort of thing as part of the responsibility and opportunity of being one of His children.

One night I came across a verse that hit me right between the eyes. It was Matthew 5:44: "But I say unto you, Love your enemies, bless them that curse you, do good to them that hate you, and pray for them which despitefully use you, and persecute you." I kept reading it over and over again. Ever since that night I've wondered if this isn't perhaps the most challenging and difficult assignment for a Christian. Let's face it: the natural, human thing to do is not to love our enemies. And how can we go around blessing folks who cuss us? How can we think of ways to do good things for people who hate us? And when someone despitefully uses us and persecutes us, it's pretty easy to overlook them when we say our prayers. But those are the very things God commands us to do. I don't read it as only a recommendation. It sounds like an out-and-out order to me. I'll bet if we took a poll of all the Christians in the world, we'd find out that this is the toughest thing in the world for them to do. It's right there in black and white: we're supposed to turn the other cheek! Sometimes our urge is to revert back to the Old Testament ways of the eye for the eye and the tooth for the tooth, but Jesus tells us, "Be ye therefore perfect . . ." (Matthew 5:48) even though he understands that we all sin and come short of the glory of God. He still *wants* us to be perfect, to give it an all-out effort every day, even though he understands when we fail and loves us despite all our faults.

So, just for the record, I hereby forgive everyone who thinks I'm downright stupid!

I know how it all got started. When some offers started to come in after my senior season at Woodlawn High, I had no idea how to handle the situation. I was a very naive kid and easily influenced. Every time a recruiter would make a pitch, I'd say to myself, "Gosh, they just can't play without me." Everything sounded great. Everyone was convincing. Someone would ask me to go to a certain school and right off I wanted to go. I didn't have a whole lot of offers, perhaps a dozen or thirteen. I could have gone to LSU, Florida State, Baylor, Texas A & M, Texas Christian, Louisiana Tech, Mississippi State, maybe SMU and a few others that slip my mind. Remember that all this happened so quickly. I had no real time to prepare for it and get used to it. It was just like an explosion late in my senior season. Till then, no one cared.

At first I thought it'd be nice to play major college ball. But down deep I knew I was scared of big-time competition. I really had no confidence in my ability. You have to remember that in my senior year I completed only 76 passes or something like that, and I wouldn't have completed very many at all if Tommy Spinks hadn't been such a terrific receiver. I'll bet if you checked the records you'd find I had 50 completions to Tommy. So it wasn't as if I was sitting back there picking defenses apart.

There was a lot of pressure from Louisiana State (LSU) alumni. It was like, "We gotta get a passer down there. We can't let a Shreveport boy get away." They hadn't done well recruiting in my area and they really went after me. Trey Prather was down there, and I didn't wanna go there because he was my idol and maybe because I thought I'd wind up playing behind him again as I did in high school. Anyway, LSU wasn't noted for putting the ball in the air that much. I went down there, and the coaches were very nice to me and I wanted to be loyal to my state school. It's an unreal thing: I loved LSU then and I love LSU now. I'll always be a Fightin' Tiger fan. I used to listen to the LSU games on the radio and went down there one time when I was a sophomore in high school and saw LSU play Tulane on a cold, windy day. It was exciting to be wanted by LSU.

A local businessman and good friend of mine to this day, Ken Hanna, really wanted me to go to LSU. He was like a big brother to me. I'd go over to his house for steaks and talk with him and his wife. I'd tell them I was going to LSU, then I'd think about it and change my mind. Then Baylor talked to me. I wanted to go there because I thought I was being led into the ministry and it was a good school for that—Baptist—and it seemed right for a kid like me. I loved John Bridgers and Don Trull. Bridgers was really nice: no pressure. I went down and saw Baylor play Arkansas. They had Trull and Elkins, and they threw the ball and I loved that. They had a bunch of high school all-stars in, and I saw some guys who had tremendous statistics. That night I was with one of the Baylor football players and he was taking a drink or two, and that shocked me. Here's a guy at a school that's supposed to be religion-oriented, and he was taking a drink. That just killed me. You have to know the background I was coming from to appreciate this. As soon as I got home, I told my dad I wasn't gonna go to Baylor, and I know that's where he wanted me to go. And I had given Baylor my word I'd come to school there.

So I told Ken Hanna he could count on me coming to LSU, and I signed a letter of intent. Then I started getting lots of pressure to enroll at Louisiana Tech University at Ruston, which is a lot closer to Shreveport than LSU. Our high school was pretty much Tech-oriented, and my brother was there and my girlfriend was going there, and I was really confused.

Now, here's how the part about my being dumb got started. I went down to LSU and took the College Boards ACT test and I flunked it. I didn't want to pass it. I took it again later on and flunked it again. I wasn't even trying. But I was such a naïve kid at the time I didn't know what I was doing to myself. How could I know then that someone would spread the word around that I was too dumb to get into LSU, just because of a sour-grapes situation and because I decided to enroll some-where else? How could I know this would be a stain on my record and follow me around the way it has?

We played the high school all-star game that summer in LSU's Tiger Stadium at Baton Rouge, and by that time I had made up my mind I would go to Tech. The LSU coaches were still trying to sell me on LSU. Then I got scared that Tech would get tired of all the fussing around and not take me. But they did. I went over, took the College Boards and passed, and enrolled at Louisiana Tech. Some of the LSU coaches spread the word that I was too dumb for LSU, and that's always made me mad, because I've always gotten good grades in school. When I was in college I went to class, I studied, and I got good grades. Back then, I was afraid that if I passed the test, it would have meant I had to go to Louisiana State. It's haunted me all my life. It may be the biggest mistake I ever made.

After our third Super Bowl victory, a good friend said to me, "Not bad for a dumb hillbilly from Louisiana."

"Not so bad, I guess. There are lots of really smart quarterbacks who never got even one of those rings."

If politics creates strange alliances, so then does professional football. It is at least curious, the closeness that exists between the Steelers' defensive tackle Joe Greene and quarterback Terry Bradshaw. It is a closeness that neither man can adequately explain and they don't try to much any longer. It's just there, that's all.

Ask Joe Greene why he has a special fondness for Terry Bradshaw, and he fidgets nervously and says things like, "I really don't know. We're not that close away from the ballpark, but there's just something about the man that brings me close to him. I guess since we started at almost the same time and more or less saw this thing through the dark days to where we are now, we're just pretty tight. I never stop to ask myself why. It's just there."

Ask Terry Bradshaw the same question, and he'll tell you that Greene is a totally selfless individual, blindly committed to the good of the team with never a thought for personal recognition. Greene, according to Bradshaw, is the consummate professional.

The two of them keep things loose in the Pittsburgh Steeler locker room. On occasion Greene will caution Bradshaw that the twang-twang of the country music is a mite loud, but it is a caution generously laced with warmth and friendship.

"Mean Joe Greene" isn't mean at all. His violence is the controlled type between the white lines of a football field. Off the field he is quiet and gentle. He had been with the Steelers one long season when the much-heralded quarterback from Louisiana Tech arrived:

"Right from the start, I didn't think of Terry as just a quarterback. He was a football player. An athlete. He was out there trying to win a ball game as an athlete would try to win. He'd do everything possible: run the ball, put his head down, whatever. He did everything quarterbacks weren't supposed to do. Right away you knew he had courage. And he was the guy who was supposed to lead us out of the dungeon. People say he and I attached ourselves to each other. I don't try to figure it out: Maybe it was selfish on my part; maybe I knew our situation rested with him. They say offensive and defensive players aren't supposed to be close, but Terry and I have always been very close.

"But I'd get mad at him, and still do sometimes. Usually it was because he'd do things quarterbacks shouldn't. He'd be stubborn and put himself in jeopardy, and he'd be putting the rest of the team in trouble if he got hurt. Mainly, though, he got his feelings hurt. The people in Pittsburgh treated him unfairly for many years. And I said so, publicly. On top of that, he was learning the game from a very tough man (Coach Chuck Noll) and a perfectionist. Chuck has a way of not showing his emotions. And Terry was a loner and needed friends, and he was getting a lot of undue abuse. From the fans. From the media. I remember one game a few seasons ago when Terry got hurt and Hanratty came in, and it was quiet— sort of split-second timing—and I heard the cheers from the fans. Now, I was there and I heard the cheers before Terry Hanratty came onto the field. There were some conflicting stories later that they really weren't cheering the fact that Brad got hurt but rather that Hanratty was coming in—but that's not true. They were booing Brad, all right. I just didn't believe it! And I said so. That crushed me so much. There was no way that could have hurt me as much as it did Brad, but it came close, believe me.

"And you know, in those early years some guys made fun of Brad a little bit because of his religion and because of that country-bumpkin attitude of his. That made me mad too. After all, he's just being himself and how can you degrade a man for being himself? It was unreal! But Terry is so sincere and has really an unselfish attitude. He'd do anything for the team. I honestly don't think it matters to him whether he does well personally, just so the team does all right.

"It's funny, looking back at Terry's career. For a long time, I think, it wasn't any fun for him. He was always looking at the sidelines and wondering if he'd be put on the bench. History probably won't record it, but I think Terry really came into his own in the playoffs in 1974. We had some tough games against Buffalo and Oakland, and then against Minnesota he called the whole game from the line of scrimmage. I mean, those plays weren't coming from the huddle. The whole game was audibles, plays called after we got to the line of scrimmage. We called 'em 'check-with-me's' because we had plays designed to run against specific defenses, and he'd go up there and call plays that would correspond to the particular defense the Vikings were showing. Things just came together.

"Then Brad started to grow as a man. He was learning the game and learning the system from a brilliant man. Chuck let Terry make his own mistakes.

"In 1976, when Terry was hurt so much, and Mike Kruczek went in to sub for him, you could see the big change in Brad. He could accept the situation for what it was. He knew he was the first-string quarterback. He wasn't worried about losing his job or not getting back in there. And he put all his resources into helping Mike be a better quarterback. Brad was fully grown. The game was fun for him, and he was at the point where he didn't have to prove himself to anyone. Now, when things aren't going the way he'd have them go in his personal life, he can put those things aside and do the job in football. He's able to take all the weight off his shoulders, and that's what has made it so beautiful for him and for me, and for the Steelers.

"There's a lot of glue that holds this team together. It's really a close group, but we don't go around with little mottoes and slogans and tricky little things written on the walls. We just have one little thing we think about and that's 'Whatever It Takes' and that's how we operate. Terry's a great practical joker and helps to keep us loose. He has a tremendous wit—he could be an actor or an entertainer. The sports world has portrayed him as a country bumpkin, a dumb country boy, and he can play that part. But he can be Park Avenue, too. He's just the kind of quarterback this team needs.

"And we have the right kind of coach for this team. The man's a genius. He's a teacher. He doesn't have to raise his voice and swear and go though all those disciplinary things, running laps and all that. He treats us like men. In ten years I don't remember that a single spirit meeting or pep talk has been necessary. We just do the job, that's all. Things are beautiful. I used to worry a lot, but I don't worry any longer. I've made up my mind that my career is going to be based on Terry Bradshaw's career. I'm gonna play as long as he does."

Prophet Without Honor

A prophet is not without honour, but in his own country. . . .
—Mark 6:4

4 The homecoming to Shreveport after Super Bowl XIII was great—for a little while. All I wanted to do was go to the ranch and relax. We had a news conference in Shreveport when we got home February 7, and for forty-eight hours everything was fine. Larry Gatlin had an appearance in Shreveport on February 9, and we had made arrangements to spend some time with him. We were together during the day on Friday, and I went to the concert with him that night. He's one of my favorite entertainers and a tremendous guy besides that, and we really had looked forward to this. But some folks spoiled it for us and left me wondering just what people in my hometown really think of me. I've heard boos in football, even from our own Pittsburgh fans; but I never in my life expected what happened that night in Shreveport. After all, that's my hometown. I'm one of them.

*T*erry Bradshaw, the hometown boy who made good, was lustily booed by the people of that same town Friday night as he made a guest appearance at a country music concert.

The incident occurred when Bradshaw came on stage with entertainer Larry Gatlin, who has written a song Bradshaw will record. When Gatlin introduced the Pittsburgh Steelers' quarterback and most valuable player of the recent Super Bowl game, a crescendo of boos cascaded through Hirsch Memorial Coliseum.

Boos were heard several times during Bradshaw's appearance on stage despite pleas for a respite. "I was shocked; I was stunned; I was very hurt," Bradshaw said later in an interview.

He continued, "I absolutely couldn't believe it—I realize this is a Cowboys' town, but gosh, it's only football. . . . This is the first time I have ever been booed (outside of football)."

Bradshaw, who is widely credited with being Shreveport's goodwill ambassador to the nation, said he was disgusted by the booing incident.

"I'm proud of Shreveport," Bradshaw said. "Everywhere I go, I talk up Shreveport, Louisiana. This is my home, but man, I just couldn't believe what happened.

"I really didn't even want to go out there, but Larry had asked me and heck, it's my hometown, so I went ahead. I was really humiliated, though," Bradshaw continued.

Gatlin, who had invited Bradshaw to make an appearance, said: "The people here showed a total lack of class. The incident ruined my whole night.

"I saw the hurt in his eyes as it happened. He's a human being, a great human being. He's got feelings just like everybody else."

Gatlin said he was a Cowboys' fan and even admitted betting $250 on the Dallas team in the recent Super Bowl, but wondered what that had to do with a music concert.

"Yeah, so big deal. That has nothing to do with Terry. For him to come here, to his hometown, and for the people to act with such total disrespect——

Gatlin said because of the incident, Friday night was his last appearance at Hirsch.

"I'm really disgusted. I'll never play here again. I am ashamed to say I was here, and I don't care if anybody in Shreveport buys my albums anymore or not."

Shreveport Journal
Saturday, February 10, 1979

KWKH Radio threw its Second Annual Listener Appreciation Show last night at Hirsch Coliseum. Well over 5,000 listeners showed up to hear the good country music of Larry Gatlin, Johnny Duncan and Charly McLain.

They also got a few surprises.

First of all, Duncan was late for his set. The word passed around backstage said his bus had some mechanical problems. Gatlin and his band went on early, which is very unusual for a headliner to do, since Duncan was still scheduled to make an appearance. Thus the headliner performed between two "opening acts."

The second and biggest surprise of the evening came six songs into Gatlin's set. Gatlin had dismissed the band for a short while and was preparing to sing a few solo songs for the crowd.

Then Terry Bradshaw joined him for a duet.

The crowd had known that Bradshaw was mingling with the performers backstage. In spite of attempts to remain anonymous, his presence became known to all those who sat in the wings. Throughout the first part of Gatlin's set, people who could see behind the stage were yelling "Terry! Terry!"

After grinning and waving to the crowd, he walked to his seat in the bleachers. Some coaxing from KWKH Ranchhands brought him down and onto the stage just as Gatlin finished his solo song "Heart."

It was totally spontaneous. Bradshaw was confused, but happy. (Backstage he made it clear Gatlin was one of his favorites. "Now you be sure to say nothing but nice things about Larry," Bradshaw had said half-seriously.)

Gatlin was also confused. After some consultation, the pair decided to sing a Hank Williams song. They settled on "Your Cheatin' Heart." The two voices mingled and sometimes faltered. Bradshaw had to be coached during some of the vocals and it was clear that he was no Hank Williams. But he was Terry Bradshaw of the Pittsburgh Steelers, and that was enough to make the crowd roar.

Most of the people shouted their approval. A few Cowboys' fans made their discontent known. Behind the applause and hoopla there was an annoying chorus of boos and jeers. At one point, Bradshaw jumped up from his seat, his cowboy hat torn from his head by his own angry hand. But the rage passed instantaneously and he grinned from ear to ear.

Bradshaw was a big man last night and he probably won many new fans.

Shreveport Times
Saturday, February 10, 1979

Gene Dickerson, station manager for Radio Station KWKH, called reports of the booing "dramatically overstated." He described Terry as "a super athlete and a genuine nice guy," but said the city got an undeserved black eye over the incident.

In an editorial, the *Shreveport Journal* commented: "Some obviously disgruntled Dallas Cowboy fans were still sore over their team's loss to the Steelers. So these backyard quarterbacks decided they'd try to do what the Cowboys could not do: humiliate Terry. Sorry to say, they did a pretty good job. The normally jovial and effervescent Bradshaw appeared afterwards to be crushed by the ugly incident. . . . Through good seasons and bad, Terry Bradshaw has managed to keep football in a healthy perspective, although players and fans alike find this harder to do every year. His simple style of living reflects a kind of rugged character that Americans still like to think lies deep down in their sports heroes. Those who booed Bradshaw Friday night should ask what kind of character lies deep down in themselves. As for the rest of us, we are proud of you, Terry. And we hope you'll find a way to be proud of Shreveport again."

Columnist Jim Montgomery of the *Shreveport Times* wrote an open letter to Terry Bradshaw which said in part:

"You may not know it yet, but you and Fate came along at just the right time to teach Shreveport a few things it needed to know about itself. . . . You see, Terry, for the past several weeks here at home we'd been going through a discussion of Shreveport's identity, its image—how a good self-image at home would help us achieve a national identity that the town needs, and conversely, how a positive national identity would help us have a better self-image. Shreveport's been down on itself for too long, and it's really hard to turn that sort of thing around, but some of us are trying. Your name came up quite often in those discussions—local boy makes good, that kind of thing—and a lot of us agreed that we were really proud of Terry Bradshaw (even if some of us were for Dallas through the season) and proud to be his hometown. . . . You've really got a lot of friends who want you to know how sorry they are this happened, and who are disgusted with Shreveport because it happened. . . . I don't know why there hasn't been a Terry Bradshaw Day for you, but that's a good example of what I was saying earlier: We've all been proud of you, but we haven't done much to show it publicly. And in our relative silence, the boos probably seemed louder than ever. . . . I'm sorry you had to be hurt, but I thank you for the lesson your experience may help teach Shreveport."

Harold M. Terry, sheriff of Caddo Parish, quickly fired off a letter to Bradshaw telling him that ". . . the vast majority of Shreveporters, including myself, consider you a credit to our city, an outstanding athlete in your field and, most importantly, a Christian gentleman." He said the incident ". . . could only represent a tiny, ill-mannered minority."

Civic leaders in Shreveport area rallied behind Terry Bradshaw. Billboards were quickly covered with signs telling passersby about Terry's accomplishments and about the area's pride in those deeds. The mayor of the city spoke out strongly in Terry's behalf. Letters to the editors of the major daily newspapers were top-heavy in defense of Terry. There was overwhelming sentiment for a "Terry Bradshaw Day" but Terry himself vetoed the idea.

*I*t just didn't seem right to me. It was too soon. Too contrived. I'm sure lots of people were upset about what happened, but remember that it happened to me. Some said those people who booed were just disgruntled Dallas Cowboy fans, and maybe most of them were. But that doesn't take away the fact that they were booing. I've always tried to represent the city of Shreveport and its people to the best of my ability.

When I was just a kid, I remember my dad and mom telling me when I was going out into the streets that I carried the name of Bradshaw with me and that we were good, proud people and we should be proud of the name and conduct ourselves in a way to bring honor to the name. I can't tell you how many times I've heard my dad say those things. Ours has always been a pretty simple family: Work hard, mind your own business, don't force your ideas on anyone else, go to church, pray regularly, and behave yourself. We were taught to respect other people and to rejoice in their successes.

But instead of rejoicing in the success that came to me, some people chose to try and embarrass me. And if I had let them rush out and put together a day for me, it would have looked as if I was a part of a movement to force myself on some people; that I was helping out an avalanche or an outpouring of support that maybe wouldn't have come about naturally. The people who really know what makes me tick and who have known me for a long time know what kind of man I am. As for the others, nothing I could possibly do would change their feelings.

First off, I have to please God. Then I have to please my family and myself. Then if there's time, I'll concern myself with pleasing others.

One Dream at a Time

5 I always had a dream, a burning ambition to play quarterback in the National Football League. But I had a dream long before that, and it was to be the starting quarterback someday for Woodlawn High School in Shreveport, Louisiana. I figured if I could just do that, then everything would be all right. But I didn't get to start until my senior year, because there was a guy a year ahead of me named Trey Prather and he was terrific. He was my idol—almost a god to me—when I was at Woodlawn High. And I didn't get the job until he graduated.

There is a stone marker bearing a plaque in the courtyard in the center of the Woodlawn High School complex. The marker stands just in front of the flagpole on which the American flag is raised each morning. On the plaque are the names of the four Woodlawn High School graduates who lost their lives in the Vietnam conflict. One of those young men was Trey Prather.

Shreveport is a city oriented to high school football. It has been said that the city has experienced two strikes—one for oil in 1906 and the other for quarterbacks. And Woodlawn High has spawned the finest of quarterbacks. The school did not open its doors until 1960. Billy Laird graduated from Woodlawn in 1962 and played one season with the Boston Patriots. Prather graduated in 1965 and went on to LSU, and they say he might have made it in the pros had it not been for that landmine explosion in Vietnam. Then came Terry Bradshaw, class of 1966, and then Joe Ferguson of the Buffalo Bills, class of 1969. The folks in Shreveport tell you that John Booty, class of 1971, could have made it too, but he chose instead to become a minister. And other NFL quarterbacks—Bert Jones and James Harris—came out of not-too-distant communities.

Ellace Bruce was Terry's first coach, when the kid was an eighth-grader in the fall of 1961. He remembers:

"He transferred to Oak Terrace Junior High from Linwood School, and I guess I'd have to say he was just another kid who came out for junior high football. There wasn't anything special about him except his enthusiasm. We had maybe a hundred youngsters or more who came out for the team and we didn't have enough equipment to suit out nearly that many. It wasn't uncommon for an eighth-grader to make the team, but most of the kids who played quite a bit were older, the ninth-graders. It was more or less a case of the youngsters coming out and getting the once-over. We'd go out in shorts and tee shirts the first two or three days just to check 'em out. We'd run through certain drills and then pick out who we thought would be the best players, the ones we thought would help us. Naturally some of the youngsters became disenchanted and dropped out, but we usually dressed sixty or sixty-five youngsters, and they all had good uniforms and good equipment because of the athletic fund we drew from in Caddo Parish.

"Terry was fairly large for his age, and he worked hard. I worked mainly with the ninth-graders, and Leonard Ponder worked mainly with the eighth-graders. It wasn't long before both of us knew Terry was going to make the team, and he played quite a bit as an eighth-grader. We played a six-game schedule, and I recall that Terry played mainly on defense as a linebacker. But he was our star quarterback the following season. We were looking for someone to play quarterback, because the young man who had played the position the year before had been moved to a halfback position. And we noticed that this young Bradshaw boy could really throw the football: we saw that in our physical education classes during the winter. But he never really had a full chance to show what he could do—very early in the season he broke his collarbone and had to sit out much of the season. He came back for the last two games, and we put in the shotgun formation to give him a chance to throw the ball.

"I recall that one time he went back to pass, couldn't find anybody open, and just kept running backwards. We kept hollering at him to throw the ball—throw it anywhere, out of bounds—and he just kept running every which way. When he was hurt, Tommy Spinks became our quarterback, and of course he and Terry became great friends and went on to high school and college together.

"My wife Mary had Terry in home-living class. She remembers teaching Terry to sew buttons on things, and he'd say, 'I don't have to know how to do that,' but he learned anyway. That was a required subject in those days, and every student had to take what we called an exploratory course for part of the year. Terry was never a disciplinary problem. He wasn't one who had to be told much. We'd tell him once and that was it. We'd practice each afternoon from 3:20 until 5:00. I always felt that if we couldn't get our work done in that amount of time, then we shouldn't keep that age group out there any longer than that. But junior high kids are the greatest! I love them because of their enthusiasm, their willingness to work, and the day-to-day improvement that one can see not only in their athletic activities but in their general attitude and behavior. It's a formative stage, and if you work it right you can be an influence for something good and positive in these young lives."

Pictures of Terry Bradshaw, Joe Ferguson, Trey Prather and other football stars from the Shreveport area hang neatly on the walls of the cubicle that serves as an office for Ellace Bruce, now the school's assistant principal. He doesn't collar every student who is summoned to his office and say, "See those guys up there? If you'd straighten up your act you might make something out of yourselves like they have!" But when he's asked who they are, he tells them—proudly. Sometimes a student will recognize the faces or the numbers and exclaim, "Hey, did Terry Bradshaw go to school here?"

Twice a month, Oak Terrace Junior High School still has a chapel service from 8:05 to 8:20 in the morning. Sometimes there are outside speakers, and other times a student will share devotions. Attendance is not mandatory, of course. A simple announcement is made, and those who want to attend can. It's just part of the tradition in Shreveport, like turning out good quarterbacks.

*I*n those days and all through high school and even into college, nothing mattered but football. My folks encouraged me. I did enough work in school to get by, but I was consumed by football. I'll bet you there wasn't a day in my life, from the time I started getting interested in football, that I didn't go out and throw that football fifty or a hundred times. More than that, probably. Tommy Spinks and I hit it off right away when we were young and he was as crazy about football as I was—still am, for that matter. We'd put on our uniforms, and I didn't care if it were raining or snowing or what, we'd be doing our thing. I may not have had a whole lot of talent, but I had plenty of enthusiasm and love for the game. And my home life was so happy at the same time. I just didn't have a care in the world. My folks were great to me. We always had a lot of fun around the house; we had our prayers and our devotions and our church life; and I just couldn't have been happier.

*S*tan Powell was the principal at Oak Terrace Junior High School. He remembers the family closeness:

"The Bradshaws are a family, and I mean a real family. Very close-knit. I watched Terry both at the junior high and high school levels and later on at Louisiana Tech, and I'd always see Mr. and Mrs. Bradshaw. One had to be impressed with their closeness, and I'm sure that's been a major factor in Terry's life.

"I've been in the educational field for a long time, and we cannot really convey to people how important a strong, close family relationship is to the growth of a child. A good situation at home makes for a good situation at school. Some folks may think it's a little corny to talk about things like dedication and discipline and devotion, but these things are vital. I think having heroes is a healthy thing. When I was a high schooler and college athlete I had my heroes—Tommy Harmon and 'Doc' Blanchard and Glenn Davis and all the others. I don't know what they were really like, but they were heroes.

"Terry Bradshaw is a hero and he's a fine example in every way. I've seen the pendulum kind of go back and forth. For example, some athletes have fallen in and out of favor. I've seen the time when an athlete was a campus hero. Then for a time the athlete wasn't a campus hero. Right now, I'm not sure if the athlete will ever be the hero he once was on the campus. We've had a lot of change in this country, and young people are different. We have so many material things now. We have so much more than we really need. Kids have so many distractions today. Schools have changed. Education has changed. You know, we're not like an automotive manufacturing company that can choose and control the quality of the product at the end by what they put in at the start and then say, 'Look, here's a nice, shiny whatever.' We can't do that in education. We have to take the product that comes to us from the home. We can't refine it much and change it and put it in at this mill, you see, and grind it out at the end. I think the first years— probably the first five, six, or seven years of a youngster's life—are the most important. And it was obvious Terry Bradshaw had a head start on lots of others because of the kind of environment he had at home."

I was pretty immature when I went to Woodlawn High. There is no way I could play right away, and I knew that. But it didn't matter. Just to be on the team was good enough for the time being. As a ninth-grader, I got a taste of what it was like to play, and then all that mattered was getting a bigger taste. My time finally came as a senior. There was no reason to think we'd have a good team, but even that didn't matter. I was such a jock, so into football. Playing football for Woodlawn High was the greatest thing in the world. I didn't know how to act; I had no idea how to *be* a quarterback; I was very shy.

Only my dear friend Tommy Spinks knew how I really was. That's because we were together almost every minute we were awake. No one else knew me, and it didn't seem as if they really wanted to know me. I couldn't figure out why people weren't friendly, and I finally discovered many years later that I wasn't that receptive: I'd try to get a story or a little joke in, and everyone would kind of ignore me. There'd be a little group involved in something, and they'd just phase me right out. I was simply trying not to be embarrassed, and when I tried to put in my two-cents' worth—well, what I had to say wasn't important. That would drive me more into my shell. But I wanted to be somebody. I wanted to be somebody special. Playing for Woodlawn High gave me that feeling.

Just to be playing quarterback for Lee Hedges was an honor. Winning was a bonus. Coach Hedges is a great coach and a great man, and somehow we pulled together a team that reached the state finals. We were 11-1-1 going into the finals, played right in Shreveport, against Sulphur. We played the game in a driving rain and lost it 12-9 when I threw an interception. It broke my heart—simply broke my heart. I cried and cried. I was miserable during the game and miserable after it was over. Nobody could say a word that would make me feel better. It seemed like the end of the world to me. The only thing that finally saved it for me was that toward the end of the season, some colleges started talking to me. Until then there was no indication anyone wanted me. I guess it hadn't occurred to me much that to realize my ambition to play in the pros it would be necessary for me to play in college.

Lee Hedges has been coaching high school football for a quarter of a century. His is an enviable record. His is a weather-beaten face, and perhaps the lines are etched there because he has kept the anxieties bottled up for all these seasons. Hedges is a stolid-faced man, undemonstrative on the sidelines, and soft-spoken. He's revered by his players and the people of Shreveport. He now coaches at Captain Shreve High School and talks openly about getting out of the business. It's not that the young men don't respect coaches these days, but that they don't respect them quite as much as they used to. Just as gentleness should not be mistaken for weakness, one should never assume, because Lee Hedges is sideline-quiet, that he is any less intense than another coach. He is a plain talker who remembers Terry's high school career:

"He came to Woodlawn High from junior high with little fanfare. He was just another kid out for the team. We didn't have the time to go out and watch the junior high school kids in those days. Still don't. But he made the team and played some as a junior—enough to win a letter. But we had Trey Prather coming back, and I've always been the kind of coach who builds pretty much on a senior-junior program. Terry probably could have played before he had the chance, but these kids always look forward to their senior year and if it's pretty close . . . and we felt like . . . well, I'm not saying it was good or bad, but we stuck with Trey. And we played pretty much a defensive and ball-control type of game that year. When we could get Terry in, he played.

"When Terry's senior year came around, Tommy Spinks played a little quarterback too. He was a good, skilled athlete and had a better ball-handling technique, but Terry had the strong arm. So in the spring, we—Coach A. L. Williams and I—decided to go with Terry. A.L. was probably closer to the boys than I was, and he helped Terry a great deal. Even though I was a ball-control coach back then—and I still am—we were trying to get more into passing. I guess I was pretty slow to come around to that way of thinking, but finally we decided to let Terry just drop back there and throw the ball. Terry could throw the football as far as one would want anyone to throw it, as far as anyone could get a man down to run under it. If we worked with him at all, it was in regard to ball handling. He was very disciplined. Of course, all the boys were, back then. Terry was a good kid. And he's a good man, now.

"We called all the plays back then, and I know Terry said something later on about not liking that. When I was a young coach at a different high school, I let the quarterback call all the plays for two years. I'm not saying I'm right or wrong, but I made up my mind after that second season that I would do the play-calling. I simply didn't have the time to sit down with the quarterbacks for three hours every day after we had been out on the football field. I didn't have the time to drill more things into them. That's cheating the boys, I know, but a person owes it to the team and the fans, the public, to do as well as he can and to win if at all possible. I felt in my heart I could better help the team by calling the plays. We've lost some games, and if I'd made a different call here and there we'd have won some of those games, I'm sure. In colleges they have more coaches, and their time is more flexible, and in the pros they're doing it for a living; but in high school the young man has his studies and his family. Well, it's just the way I coach and that's it.

"Terry really matured physically. He was throwing the javelin (setting a national record while in high school) and working on weights and he jumped from 175 pounds to maybe 190 or 195. He got strong. And he was a good runner and not at all afraid to put his head down. I think if he had gone to a college where they emphasized running, he could have made it as a runner. But at Woodlawn, what sticks out most are his great passing and his wonderful enthusiasm for the game."

Coach Lee Hedges has former players all around the National Football League, so his loyalties are divided. But even old high school coaches have heroes, too, and his is Tom Landry of the Dallas Cowboys because Tom is quiet and disciplined and a Christian. Hedges said it was all he could do to root for the Pittsburgh Steelers in those Super Bowl games against Dallas, and only the fact that he coached Terry Bradshaw in high school made it possible.

I have known a lot of guys, then and since, who blotted everything out of their lives except football. And it may seem that's what I did. It wasn't my ambition to be the valedictorian of the class, and it's probably a good thing because that's one dream I couldn't have realized. But I knew I couldn't foul-up in class: I'd catch it two places, at school and at home, if I did that. So while I wasn't a bookworm, I took care of business when it came to the classroom studies and the homework. There wasn't much else to do except study at night. By most people's standards, I probably was a pretty dull person anyway. Yet it was drilled into the Bradshaw boys that we had to behave, that we were carrying the Bradshaw name, and that we could expect trouble from Dad and Mom if we put a stain on it.

*H*is name is Joseph William Cook. He prefers to be called J. W., but most everyone calls him Bubba. He used to be the assistant principal at Woodlawn High in Shreveport, and now he is the principal. Bubba Cook makes no effort to hide his great enthusiasm for what he likes to call "the pursuit of excellence" on the athletic fields as well as in the classroom. Pictures of Woodlawn's athletic heroes adorn the walls of his office. Cook has never missed a Woodlawn football game and often wanders over to watch the Knights practice.

"I'm from a little community, Haynesville, just a little north of here. Folks there are wild about football," said J. W. Cook. "I think perhaps the fathers all passed out little footballs instead of cigars when a baby was born. Our big rivalry was with Homer, and the traditional game was always played on Thanksgiving Day. The joke used to be that if the game was in Homer and there was a fire in Haynesville, then Haynesville would just have to burn down 'cause everybody would be in Homer. And vice versa. Maybe you could say I'm more football-minded than the average high school principal.

"But even though this school didn't get started until 1960, it has quickly built up quite an athletic tradition. We've had some wonderful athletes go on to do very well in the colleges and with the professional teams. Naturally we're all enormously proud of Terry, but we're more proud of the kind of man he is. I guess I remember the game against Lafayette better than any of the others he played. It was a playoff game, and we had a long bus ride down to Lafayette. Our boys and their boys came out of the locker room at the same time, and one of their players said to another, 'Let's hurry up and get this thing over with.' Well, sir, that was a mistake. Terry had a great night, and we went on to beat them 28 to 13, and that's the game that got us into the state championship game. And I think that's when all the college scouts really started to sit up and take notice of Terry's abilities."

Where My Heart Is

*Train up a child in the way he should go: and when he is old,
he will not depart from it.*   —Proverbs 22:6

6 Some famous man—perhaps it was a woman—said
once that an apple doesn't fall far from the tree. If that
means that when I have a few more years on me, I'll
have the same character and type of life that my mom and dad
have, I hope it's true.

People say I've been lucky because of the three Super Bowl
victories, because I'm able to play professional football, because I've been able to make a good living playing a game—
doing something I really enjoy—and because I get to travel and
stay in nice places and get lots of attention. And every bit of
that is true, and I'm the first guy to tell you how lucky I am. But
I wish all who think of Terry Bradshaw as lucky could spend
just one evening around the house with my family and then
they'd see how *really* lucky I've been.

We're a tremendously close-knit family. Some who have
been around the Bradshaws may think we're too close. But
since I've matured some as a Christian and thought about a
family of my own, I've read a lot about the things that make life
good, the things that are really important down the road, the

things that keep life abundant. And most of those things are centered around the family. Maybe I'm a little old-fashioned and maybe a bit square, but I think if people concentrated more on family life, and on doing things together instead of flying off in a hundred different directions, we'd have a lot fewer problems, not only in the home, but around the world. Peace of mind—that's what it's all about. Thank God I was raised in a good Christian home with lots of love, where people care about one another, about what happens to each other, where the good times and the bad times are shared by every member of the family.

We were in church every time it was open when I was a kid. We had regular Bible study and prayer at home, and I knew both my folks were on the right track with God. I guess it'd be called an uncomplicated faith. My parents didn't push me into anything—it was just a way of life with us. We learned as much as we could handle and when I was in the fourth grade, I told my Sunday school teacher I wanted to be saved. So the next Sunday, when the minister gave the invitation, I went forward and then was baptized.

A few years later—I must have been in junior high then—I started having questions about my faith. I wanted to know more about it. The whole thing was mystifying to me. I'd see people doing terrible things and God seemed to take care of them. And I saw good people hurting and suffering and it seemed to me that God wasn't being fair. I saw a lot of people pretending to be good and they really weren't very nice at all. I tried to work it all out in my mind, and through some pretty thorough Bible reading I got a little better understanding. When I was a senior in high school, I felt the need to rededicate myself to Jesus Christ.

By that time I knew a whole lot more about my own faith and what God could do with a person's life. When we are young, there's so much we don't comprehend about God and about life in general. And there's a certain amount of emotionalism involved with being saved. I think if lots of people admitted it, they'd say they went forward or made a decision based more on fear and emotionalism than on an intellectual basis. We're afraid of God. We're guilty about sinning. We're scared of dying and going to hell. I've found that you have to study the Bible and grow in faith. If you merely accept Christ and sit around waiting for your life to change, I just don't think it's gonna happen that way. You have to work, pray, and study in order to bring about change. You have to use Christ as the example and try your best to be like him, but also understand, as it says in the Word, that you cannot possibly measure up to him. But he's set a standard for all of us, and he expects us to try. I've been extraordinarily lucky in that before I had much comprehension about who God is, I had terrific examples at home from the time I can remember.

*B*ill and Novis Bradshaw set those examples. They're not fancy people. He's the son of a sharecropper from Sparta, Tennessee, and she's the daughter of a dirt farmer from Hall Summit, Louisiana. They were born into God-fearing homes, but Bill's trouble was that he left home before he grew up.

"My folks broke up when I was nine, and there were five of us Bradshaw kids. I remember Mom taking all of us to church every Sunday, and we'd sit around and read the Bible by the light of an old kerosene lamp. We moved around quite a bit before Mom and Dad separated and we attended whatever church was close. I took a course in welding, then I went to Panama City, Florida, and began to work. I was thirteen when I left home, and I guess it was 1943 when I got to work in Florida, so I must have been fourteen then. Went to work in a shipyard. For a year I lived in an old abandoned barber shop. They were supposed to have housing for me in a barracks, but when I got there they didn't seem to know I was coming. I had two dollars and forty-six cents to my name. A fellow by the name of Worth Pennington from Birmingham, Alabama, took pity on me—he was a timekeeper on the second shift—and he found me a place to stay."

Bill Bradshaw's grandfather John was a minister around Sparta and so was his uncle John. But Bill's father sort of squandered his life away. It made such an impression on Bill that he made up his mind there'd be no squandering of life in his household.

When Novis Bradshaw was growing up, the six children

rode to church once a month in a wagon. It was uncommon in those days for the Mount Zion Baptist Church in Hall Summit to have a full-time minister, and most often the circuit preacher came once a month to occupy the Mount Zion pulpit.

"I was raised in a wonderful Christian home, but I really didn't give my life to the Lord until I was the mother of two children. It was here in Shreveport. I had a wonderful lady who taught my Sunday school class and I loved her dearly, and she was the one who led me to that decision. Mrs. Alice Joiner was her name, and I made my commitment at the Calvary Baptist Church."

Her husband made the same decision on Easter Sunday soon after Novis made her public profession of faith.

"It was in 1953," he said. "All through my time in the service I had gone to various services of different denominations and I believed myself to be a Christian. But after several prayer sessions with some good friends, I learned that what I had before didn't amount to a hill of beans. I knew I had to step out and make a meaningful commitment and accept Jesus Christ as my personal Savior. Until that time, I guess I was sort of mixed up."

The Bradshaws did not spare the rod when the three boys were growing up, but both insist there weren't many occasions when that kind of punishment was necessary. Looking back, Bill Bradshaw thinks he might have been a little too stern with the three boys. There were rules, and one of them was that you completed every task you started. There'd be no quitting a team no matter how poorly things might be going. The boys worked in the summer months.

"I've always said I didn't have the closeness with the boys that I'd like to have had," he added. "But looking back, I guess the results are what counts. And we've got three mighty nice sons."

The handsome ring from Super Bowl IX rarely is off Bill Bradshaw's finger. But the family paid heavy dues along the way.

The pressures began after Terry's senior session of football at Woodlawn High School.

"The folks from the colleges were everywhere," said his

mother. "The phone was ringing all the time and there was always somebody sitting in our living room. His dad wanted him to go to Baylor. His girlfriend wanted him to go to Tech. His dad was dead set against that. There was lots of pressure for him to go to LSU. His older brother was already at Tech. Personally I didn't care where he went as long as he was happy. Amid all this, our youngest son Craig, who was in the fourth grade at the time, was almost lost in the shuffle and we finally had to put him in the hospital for ten days. Found out later it was just nerves. But this household was in an uproar constantly. Terry counseled with the minister over his decision.

"When he finally settled on Tech, we thought it'd all be over. Then came that business about him not being happy there and wanting to leave. It was confusion all over again. We surely put in a lot of hours praying over these decisions. He'd come home almost every weekend—he's always been pretty much of a homebody. Then when everything got straightened around at Tech and he did so well, the matter of the pro draft began. Seems as if we've always had a bit of football madness around the house. But we've seen it through as a family. You know, all the awards on these walls, all the plaques, the magazine covers—they're all very nice and they're important. And we're wonderfully pleased with Terry's success, and we're just as proud of our other two sons. But I guess we don't look at all these outside things the way a lot of folks do. I'm not in awe of other people, no matter what they've acquired or accomplished in life. To have a good relationship with your children is really important. To have a Christian family, a loving family, a caring family—those things really matter. And that's what the Bradshaws have."

Backwoods to
Bright Lights

7 Once I settled on my choice of colleges, I assumed my life would take on at least the appearance of normalcy. But things got worse.

We had a bad team at Louisiana Tech and we had lots of players who didn't seem to care how bad we were. We lost seven straight games, won a game, then lost the last two. It happened that I went all the way in the only game we won, against Southeastern Louisiana. Joe Aillet had been coaching at Tech a long time, and I guess there was some pressure on him to quit. So he did, after my freshman season, and then it was madness around there. (*Terry as a freshman was 34 of 81 for 404 yards, 0 touchdown passes, and 3 interceptions.*)

The team wanted one of the assistants, George Daugherty, to become the head coach. I loved the guy. He recruited me for Tech. But I saw that Tech needed discipline and leadership, and the truth of it was, he didn't do anything to help create that sort of thing as a member of the staff. I thought they needed a whole new approach to football. I love the game and have always been willing to work and pay the price and dedicate myself to making things work. And I knew we didn't have the kind of people there to make that happen. So when they got up this petition for Daugherty, I was the only player who refused to sign it. I really caught it. Guys threatened to beat me up and everything. Some people took the petition and showed it to Daugherty's wife, and by then I was on everybody's blacklist. But I didn't care. I still love George Daugherty today, but I just didn't feel we'd get the kind of discipline we needed. Remember, I was seventeen, and who am I to say what kind of head coach he would have been? But that's what I thought, so I said it.

They went out and hired Maxie Lambright out of Southern Mississippi. I nearly died! All I knew about Lambright was that he was one of those three-yards-and-a-cloud-of-dust coaches. He was hired in the spring and we didn't have time for spring practice. Things couldn't have been more fouled up. When I went home to Shreveport for the summer all I could think about was getting out. I went immediately to A. L. Williams, who was on our coaching staff in high school, and told him I wanted to leave Tech. And I asked him to help me. I wanted a scholarship to go anywhere: "Just get me out of Ruston, Louisiana." Old A. L. understood my situation but he said, "I can't do that, Terry. I can't make any calls like that. We'll both get into trouble."

Well, someone did something, because word came to me that Florida State would take me. So my older brother Gary and I drove all the way to Tallahassee. When I called the people at the college, they wouldn't even talk to me. It was pretty obvious to me, as young and naïve as I was, that someone from Tech had made a telephone call ahead of me. "Terry, you're making a big mistake," Florida State told me. "We have no scholarship for you. We can't have anything to do with you. You've come a long way for nothing." Then they hung up.

Gary and I just stared at each other. We had gone twenty-two hours for nothing and had another twenty-two hours staring us in the face. So we just jumped in the car and came on home and I had no choice but to go back to Tech. I made up my mind to make the best of it, to play the game the way Coach Lambright wanted, and to dedicate myself to working my head off for the team.

At the start of my sophomore year, I am sharing time with Phil Robertson. He is really the number one guy, but right before the opening game, he quits. Just walks out: I can't believe it. Now I'm the quarterback: nothing else matters. We're about ready to play Delta State and someone goes and talks Phil into coming back to the team. He comes back the day before we go to Delta State and while we're warming up for the game, Coach Lambright comes up to me and says, "Terry, I hate to tell you this, but we're gonna start Phil."

Well, I just take the ball and throw it to the ground as hard as I can. And I turn and walk away. Here I have been pouring my guts into this thing and the players have been pumping me up, and Phil was out and now he's back and still number one.

But Phil gets knocked out in the first quarter. I come in and throw for about 260 yards and 3 touchdowns and we win the game 34 to 7. Everything's great! Everything's roses.

Next week we go down to play McNeese State and I don't play so well, so they pull me and put Phil in and he plays pretty well. Next week against Southwest Louisiana he starts and plays okay. Next week against Arkansas State he starts again. But he doesn't do so well and I go in and play all right. And that's the way it goes all year long: in and out. On the field, then on the bench.

(Terry's sophomore statistics: 78 completions out of 139 passes for 981 yards, 3 touchdowns, and 10 interceptions.)

When the next season rolled around, Robertson quit for good. Now I was the starting quarterback and it seemed the attitude was changing. There were more players with pride, with a sense of caring about the total team effort. Our first game was at Mississippi State, and there was no way we were supposed to win. After all, we were a bunch of backwoods kids from Louisiana, and they were big dogs in the Southeastern Conference. But doggone it if we didn't win the game 20 to 13. We had whipped a major college team! I don't even remember how I played in that game, but I didn't mess things up too terribly. Then we beat East Carolina and we were starting to believe in ourselves.

Maybe the whole turnaround in my career as a quarterback came in the third game of the season. We were playing McNeese State and I was something like 4-for-16 in the first half, with as many interceptions as completions. We were getting worked over pretty badly, and when I came into the locker room at halftime I just headed for a corner where I could sit down and cry. Here I had an opportunity to play and I wasn't handling the challenge well at all. I wanted to play well. I wanted a chance to play professional football. I was scared. The pressure had gotten to me, and I knew it. The players were unhappy with the way I was playing, and they let me know it. I was letting them down. I was crushed and intimidated. No one needed to tell me how rotten I was. I was just dropping back and firing the ball, not reading the coverage at all. Finally I got myself together long enough to put my head in my hands and say a prayer. I said, "Lord, please give me the strength and courage and the confidence to overcome this horrible handicap I have, this awful fear. Help me go out there and play the best I can in the second half and I'll give you the praise and the glory. I need your help."

I played like a man possessed in the second half. I was something like 21 out of 30 for about 300 yards and 3 touchdowns. We didn't win the game, but I was on my way. The next week I threw for about 400 yards and the week after that nearly that many and 3 or 4 touchdowns. It was simply a matter of confidence, and throwing the ball with authority. I was a different quarterback, a different person. We won our last six games and got into the Grantland Rice Bowl, where we beat Akron 33-13. They tell me that's when the pro scouts started noticing me.

(*Terry's junior season performance: 176 of 339 for 2,890 yards, 22 touchdowns, 15 interceptions.*)

I didn't play as much during my senior year because we managed to get pretty well ahead in many of the games and the coach would let other guys get some experience. We ran up five in a row before Southern Mississippi knocked us off by one point.

*T*erry's good friend James Davison, an ardent Louisiana Tech supporter and successful Ruston businessman, tells the story of hopping around the Southwest in his private plane to watch Bradshaw and Tech do their thing. In Bradshaw's senior season, Tech was 4-0 and playing the University of Tennessee at Chattanooga on a Saturday night. Tech led 35-7 at halftime, and Davison noticed that the second-string quarterback was warming up for the third quarter. Davison excused himself from his party and made his way to the Tech bench. There he told Coach Lambright they'd come all that way to see the game and surely would like to see a little more of Terry Bradshaw. Lambright gave in and allowed Bradshaw to start the second half. Before he rejoined the Tech fans in the stands, Davison whispered to Bradshaw along the sidelines, "Terry, how about one more bomb for the folks back home who came up to see you?"

On the first play of the third quarter, Bradshaw hit Robbie Albright with a 76-yard scoring strike, then retired for the night.

In reviewing the 1969 campaign in its press guide the following season, the Tech spokesman wrote:

CHATTANOOGA, Tenn., Oct. 25 — For 88 minutes midway in the first period, the lights went out due to a faulty transformer. Unfortunately for Chattanooga, the damage was repaired and nothing else slowed Tech down the rest of the night. Tech scored the first four times it had the ball for a 28-0 first period lead and the reserves took over from here. Bradshaw finished with 9 of 10 for 209 yards and 3 scores and Albright picked up 143 yards receiving. Pooky Green had 24 and John Adams 71 yards rushing.

*O*ne of the games that sticks out most in my mind was the one just after we were beaten by Southern Mississippi. I had a terrible night down in Hammond against Southeastern Louisiana. They picked off five of my passes and had us 24-19 with four minutes to play. We recovered a fumble at our own ten-yard-line and we put together one of the best drives you can imagine. We got down to their one and I got it over for the touchdown and we won the game. We won the rest of our regular season games, then got beaten badly by East Tennessee in our second straight appearance in the Grantland Rice Bowl.

I spent more time on my back than standing up that day. *(The record book shows that Terry was sacked 12 times for 143 yards.)*

There was a great feeling of satisfaction, even though we never had an undefeated season while I was in college. Still, we had turned the program around in the right way. We had pride again. And there was discipline. And I felt I had matured and learned something about playing quarterback. More importantly, I was living a good life, and my faith was really working for me, and I was working for the Lord.

This is not to say I didn't get a little taste of sin. I hadn't had a drink of liquor or beer in my whole life until I was a junior in college. I even suffered through the breakup of a long-time romance while I was in school, and though I locked myself in my room for two or three days and couldn't keep a bite of food in my stomach, I didn't go crazy and get drunk and all that. This was a girl I dated in high school, and we went to Tech together. We'd been dating for about six years and she dumped me for another guy. I cried like a baby. They finally sent for my dad to come and get me. I cried and cried. My mother just laughed. They didn't know what to do with me at school. One of the assistant coaches, Mickey Slaughter, would come to my room and make me go out and get a bite to eat. Then I'd come back and lose everything I had just eaten. After I finally went back to school, I didn't date very much the rest of my time there: all the good-looking girls seemed to be taken.

And I kept busy with my church work. Almost every Sunday I'd be out preaching in some church. Then there'd be a Wednesday night meeting and quite often a youth meeting sandwiched in between.

A publicity release dated December 3, 1969, from Keith Prince, sports information director at Louisiana Tech, included these comments in answering the question "Who is Terry Bradshaw?":

"To his family, he is a point of great pride. To his teammates, he is the quarterback, the passer, the leader who must find a way to score. To his fans, he is Superman. To sports writers who see him play, he is a clean-shaven, collegiate Joe Namath. To pro scouts, he is a future pick. In lead paragraphs of game stories, he is The Blond Bomber, Terrific Terry, The Rifleman.

"To church leaders, he is the young man whom they call on repeatedly to present their youth with an inspirational message given in language teenagers understand, and by someone young enough for them to identify with.

"To himself, Terry Bradshaw is something of a dilemma to be lived with. He carries the tag All-American, yet he admits this is an honor that must be put away in his own mind as completely as possible. He sticks out like a sore thumb, yet he is a regular guy."

(Terry's senior statistics: 136 completions in 248 attempts for 2,314 yards, 14 touchdowns, and 14 interceptions.)

Maxie Lambright didn't meet Terry Bradshaw until about two days before the students at Louisiana Tech went home for their summer vacation. Very quickly the report circulated that Terry was planning to leave Tech to enroll at another school because he assumed Lambright would stick with the ground-hogging offense for which he had become known. Lambright remembers all of Terry's career at Tech:

"Sure, I heard the stuff about him wanting to leave but I didn't pursue it. I would certainly try to influence him, but I wouldn't want anyone around if he was gonna be unhappy with the program. But he stayed and he played quite a bit for us in his sophomore year, though I'm sure not as much as he would have liked. I could tell right away he was an exceptional thrower and he was very strong. He was a fine young man but a little withdrawn. In his junior year, the job was his and he took over. I've seen talent blossom many times, but Terry's exploded. I've never seen anything like it in thirty years of coaching, and I expect I'll never see anything like that again.

"I've never been one to get too close to the players because I've felt you can't be buddy-buddy and still have the kind of restrictions you have to have to be successful. But it wasn't uncommon for Terry to come over to our house and have a bite of lunch or something. He was a magnificent person, that's all—still is, of course. In his junior year, when we'd go out for practice, other players would trot or walk to the practice field, but Terry would actually sprint. It must have been several hundred yards, yet he'd be racing to get there. It was as if he couldn't wait to get there. And he'd be there early and leave late. He would amaze me even in practice.

"We'd have words once in a while. Or I'd have them, anyway. If I got exasperated with him, I'd say something like 'Terry, what in the hell were you doing out there?' and he'd know I was displeased. But he never gave me or any of the other coaches a minute's trouble about anything. He'd just have hurt feelings. He was very sensitive. Mostly he got upset with himself. I remember one time when we played Southeastern Louisiana—I guess it was his senior year—and we won the game in the last minute or so, and Terry was in the dressing room crying after the game: he felt he had played poorly and almost cost us the game. The other players loved him. He was just as enthusiastic as he could be, and he took great pleasure in a teammate's good performance. To my knowledge, there wasn't a single bit of jealousy over the attention he got. Terry always handled that sort of thing very well.

"And my goodness, was he tough! I don't ever remember Terry not starting a ball game because he was hurt. He'd get banged up momentarily, but he'd go right back in there. He has a lot of grit. As a matter of fact, he's not only the most dedicated athlete I've ever known, he's the most dedicated human being I've ever known.

"When I first came to Tech, I wasn't aware of Terry's Christian commitment. I guess no one said much about it. But as I was around him more, I could tell he was a special kind of person. I never heard him using profanity, and he never told dirty jokes. I guess his behavior, just the way he conducted himself, called it to my attention more than anything else.

"Down through the years, I've used Terry Bradshaw as an example with other football players. Whether I was trying to talk a high school player into coming over to Tech or whether I was talking to members of our squad, I'd use Terry Bradshaw as an illustration. Mainly it was his dedication. I never had to worry about him. He was always in top condition. He didn't break curfew. He had no bad habits. And if he was gone in the summer, I knew that somewhere, wherever he was around the country, a big old tow-headed boy would be throwing that football."

Maxie Lambright recently retired as football coach for reasons of health after a dozen seasons at Louisiana Tech. In those twelve seasons, Lambright's teams won 95, lost 36, and tied 2, won six of eight conference championships and played in eleven post-season games. Eleven of his former players have gone into the National Football League.

Dr. F. Jay Taylor has been president of Louisiana Tech for seventeen years. He is a dynamic and imaginative man and has spurred extensive growth at the university. A strong advocate of a successful sports program, he remembers Terry Bradshaw as the refreshing kid who restored Tech to a prominent place in football after some down years:

"We believe in excellence in every field of endeavor and in competing at the very best level we can. Over the years, we've attained major college status and we're proud of that. We have tried very hard to schedule some of the more prominent teams—LSU among them—and most of them don't show much interest in playing us. We're most grateful for the attention focused on us through Terry Bradshaw. We feel he's been very good for the school and that the school, in turn, has been very good for him. I want to emphasize that Terry Bradshaw obtained a degree from Louisiana Tech University and, further, that he worked for that degree and *earned* it. He's proved he has the intellectual capacity to earn a degree, and we're as proud of that as we are in his athletic accomplishments both here and in the professional ranks."

James Davison, the Ruston businessman, is a member of the State Board of Trustees and an enthusiastic supporter of his alma mater, Louisiana Tech. He first met Terry Bradshaw when the young quarterback was a freshman:

"I was the Sunday school superintendent for the college department at Temple Baptist Church, and it was my habit to go through the dormitory and visit various students at the beginning of the school year. I remember meeting Terry and inviting him to visit our church. He was easy for me to talk with; we had a good visit. He would often come to church and sometimes would give a devotion. I was soon aware that he was a good, conscientious Christian young man. Over the years, we got real close and spent quite a bit of time together, and I've never seen a thing that would cause me to change my mind about him. He's the best, on the field and off.

"There were some ups and downs during his college days, naturally, and I'd always try to give him a little pat on the back when things weren't going so well. He'd always bounce back. Mickey Slaughter was the first person I know who said Terry had the mark of greatness on him. I guess that was before Terry's junior year. Mickey kept raving about his quick release, how he could really fire the ball, and how he could throw on the run, even when he was moving to his left.

"Even after turning professional, Terry kept coming back here. Sometimes he would have a meal with us. I remember his first time back after his rookie season in Pittsburgh: he and Mickey and I got out here in my backyard and threw the ball around like a bunch of kids. Later on, when Terry was on the bench and Joe Gilliam was doing the quarterbacking, some of us went over to see the Steelers play at Houston, and I believe Terry didn't get in a single play all day long. After that game, he came back here with us, and he was feeling the blues. We swam in my pool and then talked about his career. I don't know how you'd describe our relationship—certainly not like a father and son—perhaps I was more like a big brother or just a good friend. At any rate, I tried to lift his spirits and told him he knew he had a lot of God-given ability and had to stick with it, and when the doors opened again he would have to be ready. When the doors opened again, he was ready, and there's been no stopping him since."

Mickey Slaughter played at Louisiana Tech and became one of its finest performers in the 1959-62 era. When his former high school coach, Maxie Lambright, came to Tech to coach, Slaughter walked away from a checkered career as a quarterback in the American Football League. He wanted to come home. It was Slaughter who got the warning telephone call from Florida State when Terry was going to quit Tech after his freshman season:

"One night I got a call from a good friend of mine who was on the staff at Florida State and he told me that not only Terry, but his favorite receiver, Tommy Spinks, had expressed an interest in transferring there. Well, there are certain NCAA rules involved in a thing like this. First, if a player at one school makes contact with another school, then the athletic director of the first school—in this case, Tech—has to be notified. This wasn't done, and there were some other things about the situation I didn't care for. I advised my friend to tell Terry to get back to Ruston as soon as possible. They (Terry and his brother Gary) did, and we made them aware that we intended to open up the offense, which was more to Terry's liking. Meanwhile, some other people around Shreveport were advising Terry to leave, but that's another story. The important thing is that he stayed, he did pass, and he did become great. We could see it written all over him. We saw it when he started working out in his sophomore year. I had been around a lot of great quarterbacks, but I could tell he had more physical ability than anyone I'd ever seen or heard of. It didn't take a genius to see that ability. He had the God-given ability to throw the football, and in my opinion that's something that cannot be taught. It's like a fastball in baseball: you either have it or you don't.

"In other aspects of quarterbacking, he had a lot to learn. He was raw in certain areas of his overall game. His play-calling wasn't so sharp as it might have been, but you have to remember he did not have to make those decisions in high school. At Tech he called every play himself. He was very strong and also very aggressive, and he was physically stronger than most opposing linemen or linebackers we played. So he was not a patient quarterback; he tried to force his performance. He had to learn to back off a little and learn when to run out of bounds or when to try for that extra yard or when to throw the ball away. He had to learn when to throw it soft and when to throw it hard, when to hang it up and when to drill it—the things a young quarterback normally has to learn.

"We had a terrific relationship. I wasn't so old at the time, maybe twenty-five or twenty-six. I could sympathize with what he was going through as a quarterback, and I think he understood me and didn't look upon me as some old fogey. There was a natural empathy between us. He understood what I expected of him, and I in turn understood what he expected of me. We expected him to give his very best every time out, and I was to try to teach him everything I possibly could. But he had that big edge over everyone else in the world from the start, the way he could fire the football.

"I used to laugh when I'd hear or read something about Terry being a dumb quarterback. But Coach Lambright never laughed at all. It always made him mad."

*D*uring my senior year, I guess everyone in the country pretty much had heard of us. We were putting lots of points on the board (averaging more than 38 per game) and we were having fun and we were winning. The pro scouts came around and some of them talked to me, and I guess I figured I'd be maybe a second- or third-round draft choice. A kid from Woodlawn High School and Louisiana Tech doesn't let himself dream that he'll be the first player picked in the entire National Football League draft.

Confessions of a Crybaby

8 The 1978 season was the worst of my life on a personal level. But 1978 barely nosed out my rookie season for this distinction. It's difficult to say what I expected when I became a professional. In truth, I wasn't very professional at all for quite a while. I was pretty amateurish in my ways, and it's a wonder I survived that first season. There were people who wanted to run me out of Pittsburgh, and most of the time during my rookie year I probably would have joined that crowd.

There had been a lot of talk in the spring that I would be the first player taken in the NFL draft. I was at home—came home especially for the draft. The night before the draft, I got a call from Chicago Bears personnel saying that if they won the coin flip with the Steelers, they would make me their number one selection. My dad was kidding around and saying he hoped I got to play somewhere in the South, perhaps New Orleans, where it would be easy for him to come to see me.

The following day, I knew the Bears had lost the flip and I didn't know what to expect. I guess I thought I might be the second or third player taken. Dan Rooney called me about nine-thirty in the morning and told me I'd be the Steelers' first pick. The house was full of reporters and radio and television people. Chuck Noll got on the phone too and told me he was excited about having the chance to pick me number one. He said the Steelers would call me back. I had played in the North-South game in Miami but didn't get to do much, then I played in the Senior Bowl and was fortunate enough to be elected the most valuable player. That gave me some badly needed confidence. Dreaming about playing in the National Football League is one thing, but actually getting the opportunity to play is a whole different ballgame. I thought about it the whole night before the draft, and my dad and I and an attorney friend in Shreveport had done some thinking about what we wanted in the way of a contract. When we went to Pittsburgh for a meeting not long after the draft, it became apparent the Steelers had done some thinking. Let's say each side compromised and I came away happy with the terms.

The Steelers held a news conference and it was a big deal for all of us, especially me. I hadn't really been anywhere in my life. Well, we lived in Iowa for a while, but I was just in grade school then; I'd been to Monroe and Baton Rouge and New Orleans and then those trips for the bowl games after my senior season. So Pittsburgh was a whole new experience for me. I had no idea what I was saying in that press conference. Everyone was asking questions and I was just trying to please. I'm a talker. I like to talk. I had a crowd around me and I wasn't really afraid. Oh, I was uncomfortable, but still I enjoyed it. And the reporters did too. Man, how they enjoyed it! Here I was, green as grass and trying to please everyone, and they took to me like a hog to slop. All I did was answer everything as honestly as I could. I never once gave a thought to the differences in culture, the different life styles, or any of the other things that made me different from the people of Pittsburgh or anywhere else. I'm not saying I was misquoted; I'm sure all the things that were printed in the newspapers and magazines came right out of my mouth. But it's the way they came out: I looked like some hick!

I was on the cover of *Sports Illustrated*. Then *Newsweek*. Maybe the writers were like painters—they just drew what they saw. And I just said what I thought. The combination of the two made me appear pretty backwoodsy. There's no question about my lack of sophistication, whatever that is. I checked the dictionary for the meaning of that word, and it says that someone sophisticated is not in a natural, pure, or original state. Well, I was those things for sure. It also says "adulterated, deprived of native or original simplicity, highly complicated or developed, worldly-wise, knowing, devoid of grossness, finely experienced and aware, intellectually appealing."

Just taking them one by one, I don't feel I was adulterated, and nothing and no one had deprived me of my native or original simplicity. I've never thought of myself as being highly complicated, and I'm certainly not worldly-wise. That business about being finely experienced and aware and intellectually appealing is far too deep for me. Maybe chewing tobacco and being a man just naturally makes me gross, I don't know. But in those days I was young and naïve and just lettin' the words roll out. I even told the press we'd get the Steelers to the Super Bowl.

I encountered some controversy when I went to practice with the College All-Stars, getting ready for the annual game against the NFL champions. I had had some surgery for calcium deposits on my right thigh, and I aggravated the healing during the all-star workouts. The Steelers were afraid I'd do some permanent damage, and as much as I wanted to play in that game, I took the advice of the Steelers' doctor, pulled out of all-star camp, and reported to the rookie camp at Latrobe, Pennsylvania.

The veteran players were on strike, so I took it easy for a while and rested my leg. I just threw the ball to the wide receivers. It must have been three or four weeks before the veterans finally showed up, and by that time I had been able to spend a lot of time with Coach Noll, getting individual attention. It was all new to me. I really hadn't worried much before about studying defenses, and suddenly the game was very complicated.

Meantime, I was homesick. I must have called home every night.

Soon as the veterans arrived, I was pushed back to the number three quarterback spot. But I didn't get any bad treatment from the veterans. Lots of them went out of their way to make me feel at home. Earlier, when I had come to Pittsburgh for the first time, linebacker Andy Russell had me out to his house for a barbecue in the backyard and I got to meet several of the veterans who lived in the area. There is always a certain amount of harassment of rookies in any football camp, and I guess Roy Jefferson stayed on me as much as anyone. But it didn't make me mad. I understood what it was all about. They'd make me get up during meals and sing the old Louisiana Tech fight song or whatever else they wanted me to sing. They booed and threw food at me.

And they got me drunk, for the first time in my life. There was a rookie party and they ordered us to chug-a-lug beer. You had your choice—either do it yourself or they'd pour it down your throat. It didn't take much for me: about one glass and I was done for.

I figured God would forgive me for that. Anyway, I was too sick to pray for forgiveness that night. But I was extra heavy into my prayers, because I knew I was in a brand new world and much of it was overwhelming. I just prayed for strength and courage and the vision to see the will of God, and to do it. The camp was pretty interesting, though. Coach Noll cut some veterans and kept a bunch of rookies. We had lots of young and ambitious people make the team that year.

The press and the public already had taken sides in the so-called battle of the quarterbacks, Terry Hanratty and me. Fortunately for both of us, we became good friends right away. I've always liked him, and if he didn't like me he was too classy a gentleman to let on. He started the first pre-season game and I started the next one, and we won four out of five, including a game in my hometown of Shreveport. I was throwing the ball pretty well, completing more than half of my passes, and I have to be honest—I started to think it wasn't going to be so tough after all. I got my awakening during the regular season. When everyone started playing for keeps, it was a different story. There was no more experimenting, no more holding back plays. There was a lot of money and a lot of prestige on the line and everybody played like it.

We lost the opener to Houston. I got hit like I'd never been hit before. I had some dandy passing statistics—4 for 16, 1 interception, and 2 times sacked. Just beautiful! And what did the kid from Shreveport do after the game? You guessed it: he went in the shower and cried. The next week we lost to Denver, and I got belted around so much I had to leave the game. Then Cleveland beat us—3 interceptions and 7 sacks: I sure looked like a cover boy from *Sports Illustrated* or *Newsweek!* I felt like the bust of the century.

About this time the coach obviously was having second thoughts about his top choice too, because for the next game, against Buffalo, he alternated quarterbacks. I've said it publicly a lot of times in my life, and there's never been anything I've seen to make me change my mind about the two-quarterback system: I think it stinks. It's not good for the quarterbacks or the coach or the players or the fans. I can't think of a single good thing that has ever derived from the system. It causes nothing but confusion. And I was confused enough. I didn't help matters, with my attitude, not to mention a little bad luck along the way. I ran into a pro scout and started jawing on the morning of the game in Houston, and so was fifteen minutes late for the team meal. That cost me some money. But we won the game against the Oilers and my family came over to see the game and it seemed to make sense to take our day off and go back home for a little visit. I asked Coach Noll's permission, and he was good enough to let me do it. Then the airport in Shreveport got fogged in; I couldn't get out on Monday; I finally got to Pittsburgh by way of St. Louis and missed an entire day of meetings and a workout. That cost me quite a bit more money, but more importantly, it got me into the newspapers and I came off as an irresponsible, smart-alecky rookie who didn't care about his teammates.

It didn't help when we lost to the Oakland Raiders the following Sunday and I was terrible—12 for 27 with 4 interceptions and 5 sacks.

We're now six games into the season, and if I'm Moses who's going to lead this team to the Promised Land, it's beginning to look as if I'm gonna wander around for forty years before getting the job done. When Noll decided to stick with me as the starting quarterback the following week, I might have been the only person who was happy about it. If ever a quarterback turned in a performance shabby enough to turn even his most loyal fans against him—and I didn't have many loyal ones at that stage of my career except maybe a few stragglers in Shreveport and Ruston—it was the showing I made against Cincinnati. This wasn't a normal ballgame: it was a Monday night television special complete with Howard Cosell.

Before the game, Howard led me to believe we were on the air and introduced me as the number one flop in the NFL! It was a little Cosell prank, but it wasn't very funny to me, even after he told me he was just kidding around. I was shaky enough, and even a kidding introduction like that did absolutely nothing for my confidence. I couldn't have been worse if I had deliberately planned it: I completed only 4 of 12 passes. Now, I didn't get zapped by any onrushing linebackers and I didn't throw an interception—and there's a good reason for it: I couldn't get a pass near anyone, let alone my own teammates. I was terrible in my play selection, tentative, unable to make up my mind on anything. I was deathly afraid of throwing an interception. I spent half the night, it seems, looking to the sidelines to see if I was gonna get yanked out of there. It finally happened in the second half, and the coach went with Hanratty the rest of the way.

I have never in my life been more immature than I was that night. Instead of getting down on my knees and thanking God that my body was intact and that my brain hadn't been jumbled, I was an ungrateful snot! And we had won the game! I wasn't a team man. I wasn't anything. I even said publicly that I'd be unhappy if I was terrible and the team won 70-0! Can you imagine that? How selfish! And then I said I wanted to be traded.

The following day, the coach told me to cool it and not to talk with reporters about the quarterback situation. He was about six hours late with the order, because I'd already popped off again that morning. I was really feeling sorry for myself. I was looking for someone to come over and say, "Hey look, Brad, don't worry about it, baby!" But I got no sympathy at all, so I popped off about quitting football altogether—said I was thinking about going into the ministry. After all, it was something I really had given a lot of thought to over a period of years, and this seemed like the time to do it. Or at least to talk about it. Maybe I was trying another move to get sympathy: all I did was make everybody more angry with me. I was a crybaby, plain and simple. It didn't make me feel a bit better when Coach Noll explained to me that all this is part of my learning experience. I was the crybaby of the town and people were saying, "Look at Bradshaw. He's crying. He can't handle it. He can't take it. Hanratty's our man. He never cries when Bradshaw is playing." And they were exactly right. I had dug a pretty deep hole for myself and I had no idea how I could get out of it.

I was twenty-two years old. I didn't know a whole lot, but I understood that the quarterback is always in a love-hate relationship with the fans. I understood that if I played well, they'd cheer. And if I played poorly, they'd boo me out of the stadium. But the booing in the Cincinnati game—at home, before a national television audience—was the first booing I'd ever heard directed at me. It nearly wiped me out.

Hanratty went all the way the following week and I watched the whole game from the sidelines as we beat the Jets. Then he had an off day against the Chiefs and I came in and finished up and did fairly well. I got the start the following week and flopped and Terry came in and relieved me. It was like a revolving door. We both played the next week and beat Cleveland. The game the following Sunday against Green Bay was a nightmare. I had more interceptions—4—than I did completions—3—and I put the ball in the air 20 times. Bart Starr tore us apart, and every time the Packers got the ball, I stood there in utter amazement watching a thoroughly professional quarterback. He was making all the right moves, making all the correct calls, doing all the things one has to do in order to win. And every time I got in there, I was doing all the things one has to do to make the other team win.

Here's a guy who had been my hero, not just because of his remarkably good football skill, but because I knew he was a dedicated Christian and a gentleman. I got to meet Mr. Starr after the game, and he was really nice to me. He told me I had a lot of talent and that I shouldn't lose patience. He said it takes time. Trouble was, I didn't know how much time the Steelers were willing to give me. I remember being so impressed by him that I was afraid to call him by his first name—I thought he'd figure I was a fresh kid.

Coach Noll stuck with the two-quarterback system the following week against the Atlanta Falcons, and Hanratty got us a 16-10 lead at the half. Then I blew it. I was almost as pitiful against the Falcons as I had been against Cincinnati and Green Bay. Another outstanding performance from the number one draft choice: 3 for 12 for all of 30 yards. And *only* 2 interceptions this time. No wonder the fans were screaming! I wasn't doing a thing on the field to win them over and wasn't saying anything off it that would win friends and influence people. Noll did the fans—and me—a favor by letting Hanratty go all the way in the last game of the season. The Eagles beat us, but I was pressed into service as a punter when our regular kicker, Bobby Walden, was injured. I didn't show any better stuff as a punter than I had been doing as a quarterback. My first one was blocked for a Philadelphia touchdown. The next time, I was in such a hurry to get the ball away I kicked it a grand total of seventeen yards!

It was a perfect climax to a miserable season. All I could think about was going home. I couldn't get there fast enough. But once there, I called Dan Rooney and told him, "Don't worry, you didn't waste your draft choice. I'm going to prove to you that I deserve to be your number one draft choice." And I never worked harder in my life than I did during that off-season. I'd throw the football to Tommy Spinks, to my Uncle Bobby, to anyone who'd run and catch it. I'd be dog-tired and I'd think about all that booing and I'd throw some more.

When I went to camp the following summer, I walked through the coaches' meeting room and looked at the depth chart and noticed I was listed as the number one quarterback. I can't put into words what that did for my confidence. It was a tremendous shot in the arm. Even after all the fouling up I had done the year before, they still had some confidence in me. By then, the club had brought in Babe Parilli as an assistant coach.

He was someone I could identify with right away. He had been down that road himself; he'd had his ups and downs.

Parilli didn't do anything with me as far as technique is concerned, but he did an awful lot for me in other ways. He just kept talking to me. He explained to me what was happening and why. He told me to accept what was happening, try to work harder, and not let so many things get me down so easily. He tried to make me understand the ramifications, the ups and downs of the position of quarterback. It was an exhilarating, sharing experience, and I'll remember it as long as I live. I was like a sponge, soaking everything in. Just piling up that knowledge.

In my second season—1971—we didn't set the world on fire. We won only six games, but I threw the ball with more authority and confidence. For a still-green kid who had his confidence shot out from under him as a rookie, I think I made some important strides as a National Football League quarterback in my second season. Maybe it was the feeling that I really had nothing to lose, because I had lost it all in the first year. I'd read and heard all the stories about first-round draft choices and Heisman Trophy winners becoming big bustouts, but I had made up my mind that if I failed, it wouldn't be because I was lazy. I'm not much on statistics, and records honestly don't mean a thing to me; but someone pointed out to me that in the last half of my rookie season, I completed only 33 percent of my passes. Three-for-ten may be good enough to get a baseball hitter into the Hall of Fame, but it's the pits for a quarterback in professional football.

In 1971 I more than doubled the number of completions I'd had as a rookie and I more than doubled the number of touchdown passes I threw—even though I was still getting intercepted a lot. I wasn't out of the woods yet, by any measuring stick, but I didn't feel I was buried so deeply I couldn't see the daylight.

Andy Russell is bright, articulate, warm, outgoing, and successful. As a linebacker for the Pittsburgh Steelers for many years, he played with the kind of professionalism others should use as a standard. He played on a lot of losing teams in

Pittsburgh and remembers when Terry Bradshaw arrived:

"He had come to town and there was a lot of publicity and I wanted him to get to know some of the veteran players. Like most veterans, I was skeptical of any rookie's capacity to make a major impact in the National Football League, at least right away. It was being said that he was going to be a starter as a rookie, so I decided to host a little gathering in my backyard.

"We were a very close-knit group in those days—actually closer together, I'd say, than we were when we finally won the Super Bowl. Maybe a psychologist would like to make a study of that, but I think when you're losing, you're bound together in your misery. You feel as though people in the city don't like you. You don't have the public seeking you out. You feel as if you have your back against the wall. It's like you against the world. We had a group of great human beings, thinking guys; we just didn't have enough talent overall to be a winner.

"When Brad came out, we all immediately liked him. My impression at the time was that here was a young man who felt a tremendous burden to be something he wasn't. Maybe it was a macho image that he tried to convey. I knew right away he was walking a very difficult line because he'd probably read about Bobby Layne and people who had traditionally led the Steelers. But it was awkward for Brad. He was just too clean-living, too straight a guy. He wasn't being himself. It's not a knock against him, but he was trying to impress us, and frankly, he carried it off quite well. But the real key with him, as with anyone else coming into the league, is what happens when the man walks onto the field. It's what a person does there that counts. Brad immediately showed a talent that I can only describe as awesome. He had it from day one, and all he needed was the maturation process.

"When he first started out, Brad would make bad judgments, like anyone else. He was probably trying to do too much and trying to force things to happen. He needed to make the quality judgments. And in those days, the Steelers had many problems. First, we had a lot of very communicative guys who lived by the axiom that if you do well in football, it's because you're trying hard—and if you're doing poorly, it's because you're not trying hard enough. This is the simplistic judgment an athlete is taught from the time he first puts on a uniform, and it carries right on through to the professional level. Coaches tend to think, 'Well, it can't be the coaching.' Therefore, the players' attitudes must be bad and they must not be giving enough effort.

"Another problem was that we kept second-guessing ourselves as players. We had all sorts of team meetings and spirit parties. We'd get together once a week or so and sit and discuss how we could become a better football team. Oh, it was frustrating! We'd drink some beer and talk and commiserate with each other and of course everybody felt it wasn't his fault—it was somebody else's fault. Probably the offense blamed the defense and the defense blamed the offense. It was not to be suggested that we didn't have the talent. But it occurred to me that we just didn't have enough stallions running around: that was our overall problem. Subsequently I've seen guys come in who have not had the greatest attitude. But they had the talent. So we'd go out and dominate people, and outsiders would say 'Gee, they must have a great attitude. They must really be close-knit.' In truth, the attitude might have been better when we were losing. But when we obtained talent, we became very businesslike. We knew what we had to do, and we went out and did it.

"Now, Terry had a great attitude. But the main thing he brought to the Pittsburgh Steelers was talent. In the early years there were some difficult times: Coach Noll would change quarterbacks, and I'd sit back as a player and try to analyze that. Changing quarterbacks is a major step. Noll would stick with Terry through some tough games where Terry had made some bad judgments—maybe the offense wasn't forming. Generally I could understand why the coach did what he did. But I could understand Terry's insecurity, the feeling he had that if he didn't do well, he was coming out of the game. Early on, he took himself far too seriously and didn't have the knack of making fun of himself. He seemed to acquire that. He recognized the trick of taking some of the pressure off oneself by self-deprecation. He became pretty cute at it, as a matter of fact.

"Terry always had infectious humor, though. He was a

nice guy, and everyone felt warm toward him. All he had to do was to learn the business of football well enough to utilize that enormous talent of his. During those difficult days, we'd have dinner together—some of the veteran players and Terry—and we'd try to make him feel, 'Terry, you're one of us. If you make a mistake, realize that we all make mistakes. No one plays perfect games.' One of the keys to being successful in anything, I think, is to be able to say 'Okay, I blew it' and go on from there. In pro football, and in the quarterback position especially, you have to have a thick skin. We tried to give Terry confidence, but confidence isn't something you can give to somebody by conversation. You have to go out and get it on your own. I think he did that, and we could see his maturation each season. We could see him make fewer bad judgments and, when things would go badly and there was tremendous pressure, we could see him develop amazing concentration. It seems that the longer you play the game, the wider and longer the field becomes. It opens up. I think it has opened up beautifully for Terry.

"There are some similarities between the position of quarterback and that of the linebacker. You're trying to recognize as many keys as you can. When you're young, you just don't do it. You concentrate very hard and say to yourself, 'I've got to see the outside guard.' Then you see him, and he blocks down and you're supposed to close, but you also forget there are six other things that look the same. And you don't recognize all the other keys. It's frustrating when you're young and trying to cram in all that material. I'd say it took me eight or nine years before I really matured as a linebacker. But the pitiful thing is, you can't play linebacker much past the age of thirty-five or so, because your body starts to cave in on you. You get to the point where you know you have a feel for what's going on out there, and it helps enormously. You have a tremendous edge, but the compensating factor is that once you've reached that point, your body is giving out. Maybe there are a couple of years when your physical matches your mental. Then it goes the other way.

"Terry has spoken of how he worried about fouling up. He thought other players were thinking that if he didn't mess things up we'd be all right. That's what I was thinking too—about myself: 'Well, we can win this game if I don't give up a touchdown pass to some guy.' We're forever into that kind of psychology. We have to worry about making mistakes. And we never really quit worrying.

"But Terry really shouldn't worry. He has the most extraordinary talent of any quarterback I've ever seen. No one else is close to him. Many times I'd stand behind the offensive huddle during a workout, and he'd be performing against our own defense—the best pass defense in football. He would start to do something, and I'd say to myself, 'Don't do that! There's no way you can get it in there! There's not enough room!' I'd swear it was bad judgment and the ball was gonna be picked off; but he'd zing it in there and complete the pass, and I'd stand there and shake my head. I'd stand five feet away and watch it and still not believe it. I'm out of the game now, but I still watch him do things and I still don't believe it. He's the best: no question about that. But above his talent is the fact that he is a good, very decent human being who cares deeply about people. That's what makes Terry so special."

Ray Mansfield was the center on a number of mediocre football teams and had been with Pittsburgh the season when Terry Bradshaw arrived. Ray had begun to wonder what being a winner felt like:

"I had come to the Steelers in '64 and we kept finding new ways to lose. It's not that we weren't giving 100 percent, but near the end of the game we may have had a tendency to quit too soon. Perhaps we didn't fight to the bitter end. It's a big problem to turn losers into winners. When Chuck Noll came in to coach the Steelers in 1969, I became totally confused; I couldn't figure the man out. We won our first game, then lost thirteen in a row. But the coach never blew up. I had played under Buddy Parker and Bill Austin and Joe Kuharich and Nick Skorich—guys who were always yelling and pulling their hair out and screaming—but Noll never blew up.

"We kept blowing game after game. It was unbelievable how we lost some of them. But Noll stayed calm. He seemed to have some sort of overall game plan in mind for the club, even though he didn't articulate it. He communicated little. I said to myself, 'This man is either insane or he doesn't know what is going on.' I mean, he didn't get angry. He didn't blow his top. He'd give a little pep talk after the game and tell us to hang in, reassuring us we were gonna get it all together.

"Brad came in Noll's second season, and I think it was about midway through the year that I thought the coach had something. He definitely had a plan and knew where he wanted the team to go. It was a matter of turning losers into winners. And the first time you win, you're almost surprised and you don't know how to behave. I remember that get-together at Andy Russell's house. Brad wanted so much to please all the veterans. He came there . . . nice kid—that's the first thing I thought—what a nice kid! Terry must have told a hundred jokes. He wasn't a cocky kid; he didn't come to the team acting the way you'd expect a number one draft choice to act. We all liked him right away. This may sound a little corny, but when I look back on it, I guess we felt the way the Jews must have felt when they heard Moses was gonna lead 'em to the Promised Land. For the first time, we felt we had a legitimate, talented prospect.

"We didn't know it at the time, but later on we came to refer to a certain game in 1969 as The Bradshaw Bowl. The loser of the game got the top draft choice. We lost and we got Terry. It's probably the best game we ever lost.

"As for all that stuff about Terry being dumb—it's a lot of rubbish! People don't understand, and never will, exactly what's involved in learning first the team's system and then your way around the league. In his early years, naturally Terry didn't always find the number one receiver right away, he'd feel the pressure, and he'd look away and start off on his own. He was looking to run the ball too quickly. This happens with all quarterbacks, but it was especially true with Brad. Because he was so strong, he wasn't afraid to run with the football, and I think his size and strength were a hindrance. He was anxious to scramble. He liked it. He never minded the contact, and he never griped about getting his lumps.

"But the major thing about Brad is that he's the most unselfish quarterback I've ever known. His main concern has always been the team. This isn't just a façade—I really believe that the man cares only about the team, first, last, and always. If he drew some recognition along the way, okay, but it never has seemed important to him.

"I guess the worst season was in '74. He was in and out and Gilliam was in and Hanratty was in and everyone was confused. Terry was down and out and mad at the coach. One day I took him aside and told him he was gonna be a winner and the minute he became a winner all these people were gonna be on his bandwagon. We were in the back of the bus going to the airport in Cleveland—I remember it as if it were yesterday—and I was trying to cheer him up. I told him to ignore everybody, to go out there and do the job you're capable of doing and if you louse things up, then you louse things up, that's all. You're always going to have detractors, no matter what. I think Terry turned things around that year.

"In the earlier years, however, there were some hairy times. They seem funny now, looking back, but there was nothing funny about them at the time. I remember Brad being so upset in the huddle that he couldn't call a play. One time in Houston, when we still had a chance to win our division, we were down three or four touchdowns late in the game and backed up almost to our goal line. It was something like third down and twenty-seven to go and Terry called a sweep! I got so mad I screamed at him and said, 'Throw the ball, Terry!' Then I thought, 'My God, what did I do?' This look came over Terry as if he were saying 'Even my teammates are turning against me.' I was sorry I had said anything. It must be the way a captain feels when his soldiers turn against him. Anyway, Terry took about three steps back and then took off running. There was no way he was going to put the ball up. I guess he wanted to save himself one final humiliation; he didn't want to risk another interception. He'd been trying to force things to happen all day.

"But people forget that Chuck Noll in effect said to Terry, 'I'm going to teach you how to be a quarterback,' because from the very beginning, the coach let Terry call all his own plays. One time we were playing Atlanta in a Monday night TV game, and I told Terry to call a pass play. I thought I could read a certain defense. I wanted a 98-lead, where the running back is sort of fired past the quarterback and the center goes out as on a screen pass, and all the action is going the other way. It's a kind of weak screen pass or something. So Terry called it, and the thing was intercepted by the defensive end. When I got to the bench Noll barked at me, 'Mansfield, limit your play calling to the running game!' I never called another play for Brad.

"One time in his rookie year we played a pre-season game against the Patriots in Terry's hometown of Shreveport. It must have been ninety-five degrees, and the humidity made the temperature seem twice that high. It was in the middle of July. I'll never forget it: it may have been the heat or the nervousness or a combination, but whatever—Terry got into the huddle and he threw up. He threw up all over the shoes of the linemen.

"It took a long time for Brad to be accepted in Pittsburgh. I live here, you know, but this is a tough town. I played in Philadelphia and it is said they boo the little kids who don't find eggs at the Easter egg hunt, but there they give you a chance. Pittsburgh is tough, and Terry went through some bad years here. I don't claim to be a seer, but I said before the 1978 season that it was going to be Terry's year. You could tell: he took charge.

"Something that's great about the Steelers is that they are a tight team. Very close. They won't get complacent—it's too good an organization. What's more, we're a team that's maybe 50 percent black and 50 percent white, and we've never had any race problems. Perhaps that's because of Brad and Joe Greene. The team's a family, and a good one. Terry used to feel he was carrying all twenty-two guys on his back. But when we won our first Super Bowl, it seemed to relax him. He gradually took control of the team. He has said he didn't really feel a part of that team, but I can tell you that all the other guys felt he was. With him in there, we always felt better. We'd see him take a hit to get an extra yard, and we knew he was working extra hard for the team. We were always worried about him getting hurt, yet it was good to know he could scramble and get the job done if he had to do it. In the early years, it was as if he had very little confidence in his passing. He felt that everyone was down on him when he threw an interception. But that isn't true. Now he believes in himself. He's willing to put the ball up anytime. He likes to pass the ball. He has the confidence that comes with maturity."

Rocky Bleier joined the Pittsburgh Steelers in 1968, missed the 1969 campaign because of a graver campaign in Vietnam, then returned to the club in 1970. He remembers when Terry Bradshaw joined the club:

"It was a difficult time for all of us. The club had been down for many years, and everyone was saying that Terry was going to be the savior. He was a big, strapping kid with that close-cropped blond hair, the square jaw, and the dimple in his chin. He was as nice as can be, and everyone knew he could fire the ball. He was so full of enthusiasm. He had brought all the college rah-rah stuff with him, but instead of resenting it, the guys took to him right away. He sold everyone because of his sincerity and his eagerness to please, plus his great willingness to work. He cared about people. For me, it was a time of trying to readjust to civilian life and win a place on the team. So my thoughts were pretty much turned inward. After all, there were lots of people who thought I couldn't make it, and it was a strenuous time for both me and the club.

"It's understood in football that the quarterback can't have a bad day. As a runner, I can have a bad day. Franco Harris can have one. The coach can. But the quarterback isn't allowed that luxury. He's the guy out there in front of everybody, and the barometer: it's generally true that as the quarterback goes, so goes the team.

"At the time Terry joined us, we all were having bad days. I was playing only on the special teams then and had little input. Everyone was in Brad's corner, though at the same time we understood the unbelievable pressures on him and the additional pressure he put on himself by wanting so desperately to succeed. Coach Noll was relatively new to the job, and he was trying to get his philosophy going, and Terry was trying to establish himself, so these were trying times. Brad was his own worst enemy. He'd punish himself severely when things went wrong. The fans were on him, the press was on him, and *he* was on himself. The fans had heard and read so much about him that they expected miracles. They were comparing him with Bart Starr and Johnny Unitas and Bob Griese and established quarterbacks. He was just learning! It wasn't fair!

"Terry was really nervous. I guess I wasn't much different. I'd heard so much about Bart Starr, and when I finally met him I called him 'Mr. Starr' and he said 'Call me Bart.' No one can possibly understand the strain that's on a young player unless he's been in that situation himself. And for a quarterback, it's twice as hard. Terry had a lot of responsibility on his shoulders. The coach was letting him call all his own plays and, let's face it, Coach Noll isn't all that communicative. Here was Terry, reaching out for approval, desperately needing someone to say, 'Hey, Terry, you're my man. It's all right.' Though the players were strongly behind Terry, that wasn't enough. He had to hear it from the head man. Instead, he was hearing nothing from the coach and getting lots of flak from the fans. And he took each thing as if it were the end of the world.

"One time I was asked about Brad's play-calling, and I blurted out an honest answer, as I generally do. I said he sometimes seemed uncertain in the huddle and his play-selection was tentative. It got into the newspaper, of course, and it didn't come out exactly the way I meant for it to come out, and Brad was upset. He asked me about it. He was more hurt than mad, and I apologized to him. But he *was* uncertain, because of all the factors working against him. He's always been a guy who wears his heart on his sleeve. There's no deceit to the man. He's no con man.

"During the 1978 season, we all knew Brad was torn apart inside because of the separation from his wife and the miles between them. You see, he's not a complicated person at all. You know when things are right with him and you know when things aren't. Everyone knew he was a lonely guy: there was no secret about it. He'd run to New York to see Jo Jo for a few hours and he'd run back. He'd wonder if she was going to come in for a game so he could spend a few hours with her. But he amazed me the whole year long. He matured in every way.

He was able to separate his personal life from his professional life, and once he got to the field he was able to concentrate 100 percent on football. That in itself is a great tribute to the character of the man.

"I have always liked Brad, but until I became a starter four or five years ago I didn't know him very well. The more I've been with him, say, as an equal, as a man who knows he's contributing to the club, the closer I've been to him. I have seen him develop and grow as a football player and as a human being, and the Steelers are his football team. He's our man and everybody knows it now. And Terry doesn't have to hear it from anyone: he knows it. Because of that, the Pittsburgh Steelers won't get fat and lazy and complacent. Winning three Super Bowls just makes us want to win four of those things."

Life in the Fishbowl

When kids are little, their first choice in sports is to play two positions—quarterback on the football team and pitcher on the baseball team. When you're little, chances are the best athlete is playing those positions. How many times have you seen it happen in Little League that the pitcher is also the best athlete on the team and batting cleanup?

I've heard it said, and I suppose it's true in some cases, that in major league baseball, the pitcher sometimes isn't a good athlete at all. Quite often what happens is that the pitcher hasn't been doing much hitting for a few years, through the minor leagues and all the time he's been in the majors. They even have a guy hit for him in the American League now. And when you don't hone your skills, you can lose them. That happens to quarterbacks too. Maybe they were pretty fair runners in high school and college, but by the time they get to the pros they're told, taught, and sometimes ordered not to run. The story is told about John Henry Johnson sometimes heading for the sidelines when he was carrying the ball; someone asked him why he did that, and John Henry just told 'em that carrying the football caused him to draw a crowd. Well, a quarterback draws a crowd too—and very quickly.

Quite often the mark of an experienced quarterback, one

111

who has poise, is the amount of time he holds onto the ball before releasing it. The quarterback who can be patient enough for lanes to open and receivers to clear will be more successful. I played a long time before I had poise and I suffered for it, and so did my team. Now I think I have poise. I'm not saying I have an over-supply of it, but I've learned patience back there.

A quarterback needs patience more than anything else. The biggest reason is that he must understand he's living in a fishbowl. He's noticed when no one else is. And defensive backs get noticed usually only when they've been burned on a play. For a long time, before broadcasters began announcing the uniform numbers of players guilty of rules infractions, offensive linemen complained they were the most anonymous performers in the game. Many's the time I would have traded positions with them.

There are many things that the average football fan cannot comprehend about the game. Sometimes a fan will say, "So and so didn't make many tackles today," but he doesn't realize that so and so was double-teamed and that's what enabled the guy next to him or someone else to get through to the quarterback. The same thing happens with linebackers and defensive backs. Maybe they're covering for someone else. Maybe there's been a mistake or a missed assignment, and the guy in the stands doesn't know just who made the error: all he knows is what he sees—or thinks he sees. Football sounds like a simple game, and in some ways it is, because in almost every case, the team that does the best job fundamentally—does the best blocking and tackling—will win. For the most part, however, it's actually a complex and complicated game. It grinds me when I hear or read that someone thinks the game is played by Neanderthal men who don't know which end is up. I've found in almost ten seasons in the league that the better players are the more intelligent players—and there are many of them.

No position is blown out of proportion more than that of the quarterback. It's been said a million times, I'm sure, but it's flat-out true: The quarterback gets too much blame when his team loses, and far too much credit when his team wins.

And he has to understand that and accept it. He doesn't have to like it, any more than he has to like a lot of things, but he must know that's the way it is.

One of the toughest things a professional athlete has to adjust to is a new relationship with the media. Let's face it: for high school athletes and generally for college (though perhaps not as much now as earlier), the press is pretty rah-rah about things, and not much is said or written that's critically negative. But when an athlete gets to the pros—well, he doesn't forget that he's being paid to do a job. The press is being paid to do a job. And these two jobs can meet head-on. Once you become a pro, you get booed by people in the stands and, in much the same way, you get booed in the newspapers and on television.

I've been burned a few times for saying exactly what was on my mind, for being open and candid and myself. I haven't always liked what was said about me. I've thought to myself at times that honesty really isn't the best policy, and I've been mad and hurt and said, "Okay, that's it. No more interviews. No more anything." But I've never really meant it or stuck with it. My problem is that I like people. I like news reporters, sportscasters, magazine people: I like 'em all. They're people, and they're going out of their way to do a story on you and you want to be accommodating and friendly. I want to oblige them and give them a good story, and I want to make it interesting. I want mostly to be myself.

I think I have a good working relationship with the press. They're my friends, not buddy-buddy, but friends. I realize that when I play poorly, these friends of mine are going to say bad things about me. That's expected: I accept it and hold no hard feelings. You learn to live with that. And you learn very quickly that the media are very influential and go a long way toward determining what the folks out there think of you. Most of the fans, 999 out of 1,000, never meet you, so all they really know about you is what they hear or see or read on radio or television or in the newspapers. And the media can have a great deal to do with a team's performance or an individual player's effectiveness. I'm certainly not coming out and advocating a palsy-walsy relationship between the team and members of the working press, and I'm not saying these people should write only what makes the team look good—it's ridiculous even to think that way—but I think somewhere along the line it's good to have a mutual respect and a situation wherein there's trust.

Quarterbacks get far too much publicity. When people mention the Oakland Raiders, everyone talks about Kenny Stabler. Mention the Rams, and everyone comes up with the name of Pat Haden. It's the same with almost every team.

When I look at films or watch a game on television, my eyes are on the quarterback. And I'm looking mainly for one thing—poise. The best in my mind is Bob Griese of the Miami Dolphins. He's the quarterback I'd want in there if I had one game I had to win. He's very intelligent and very cool and never seems to get rattled. If he ever does, he hides it extremely well. I believe in my heart he's the best playing the position today, and I admire him a great deal. This isn't to say he has the best arm or that he runs fast. It's a matter of getting the job done.

Stabler is a great quarterback. He's lost some of his mobility, but he's just magnificent. I've read about that trouble he had down in his hometown, and I'd hate to think Kenny had anything to do with that.

Kenny Anderson of the Cincinnati Bengals is a great quarterback too. Besides that, he's polished, a wonderful man. I respect and admire him because I know he's a Christian.

Pat Haden's a lot like me in that he's always gonna have to fight that thing about being too short. I'm too dumb and Pat's too short. He's a gifted, poised quarterback with everything in the world going for him. He has all the tools to play extremely well. Look at the records: this past season was only his third, I think, in the league and he threw for something like 3,000 yards. You just don't do that without a lot of talent, I don't care who you are. The more playing time he has, the more experience he gets, the more confidence he will have. Whether you're a Rhodes Scholar or Phi Beta Kappa or what else, you still have to learn the game and you only learn it through playing it.

The Dan Pastorini situation in Houston is one I can really

sympathize with. Here's a guy with a great arm, but people didn't appreciate him as a quarterback until Earl Campbell came along and took some of the burden off the quarterback. Campbell's presence to the Oilers is like Franco Harris's with Pittsburgh: it lets the offense do so many more things. Dan's had some personal problems, but I think he's starting to perform with a lot of confidence. I think he's one of the great ones now, and I predict that everyone will think that in the next season or two.

I talk a lot about poise, but I think having poise is at least as important as having the good arm. And the guy with more poise than anyone else is Craig Morton. I've never seen anyone stay in the pocket the way Craig does. I've seen him actually get tackled at the line of scrimmage while he's stepping up. He just keeps stepping up to get away from people and all the time he's looking downfield. I've always been a big fan of Craig's, and since he found peace of mind by finding peace with God, the change in his life is obvious by the way he performs. He's a friend of mine and I'm proud of it.

I love watching Roger Staubach play. What a great competitor and fine family man he is. He's a remarkable human being, very intelligent, keeps himself in top condition. Roger has a keen awareness of the world, and his world is far greater than the dimensions of a football field. Not long after Super Bowl XIII, Jo Jo and I went to Dallas to take part in a conference involving Christian athletes, and naturally Roger was a part of it. I was exhausted, drained, both physically and mentally. I had been on the go night and day. When Roger and I were in Los Angeles for the Pro Bowl, we talked about the upcoming conference, and Roger invited us to have dinner with his wife and family.

When we got there for the conference, Jo Jo and I were intending to get spiritual food from the other Christians. We received some counseling about the problems we faced, and we shared our faith—and our problems—with wonderful people. I know we both gained a whole lot from that, but still I was just plain out of gas in every way. I was tired of football, tired of pressure, tired of traveling, tired of people pulling me in a hundred directions, tired of interviews. Just tired, period.

I had told Jo Jo, "Honey, this is it. I don't think I can play anymore." She just smiled.

That night with the Staubachs, I told Roger how I felt and, believe me, it did a world of good just to talk things over with him. To know that I was in the presence of not just another quarterback who's been down that road and who understands the way things can pile up, but most importantly, to know that I was dealing with a compassionate human being, a man who has a meaningful relationship with his family, a man who's a super Christian—well, it was far more than I deserved that night. But Roger understood exactly how I felt. He said that when you really have nothing left to prove, you have to ask yourself why you're staying in the game.

Here's a guy who's proved it all for a long time. I'm sure Roger is financially set. But he stays in it because of his great love for the game. He understood that night that it was my fatigue talking. He had been through that post-Super Bowl letdown experience, and he knew I was going through an unreal part of the world. Here I was, dumb old hillbilly Terry Bradshaw—now a smash hit with the media, now the most valuable player, now smart and maybe even brilliant once in a while, running around getting awards, gonna be an actor and a singer and all that—and all I wanted to do was go to my ranch down in Louisiana and collapse.

Jim Zorn, the fine young Christian quarterback for Seattle, showed up and we all talked for a while. It helped to get things off my chest. Mostly it helped to be around other Christians, who know that this world is just a stopping-off place and that God has a better world waiting for those who love Him and who are called according to His purpose. A person's real problems start when he begins to think that this world is everything and forgets that no matter how good or bad things get here, the home that's waiting for us over there is beyond description. When I'm on top and riding high—the way I was this past year—I think I'm more aware of my faith. When I wasn't so strong a Christian, I'd tend to forget about God when things were going really well. Maybe I thought I got all those good things on my own and didn't need Him. The more I've grown as a Christian, though, the more I've come to realize that I need God with me every day, not only to make me realize where the good life comes from, but to help me withstand the temptations that the world presents.

When I stand back and take a long look at Roger Staubach, I see him as a complete human being. Sure, a great football player. But so much more than that. Because of the great qualities he has as a man, he'll be able to function and thrive when it comes time for him to walk away from the game. He gives football more than 100 percent effort and at the same time he realizes that it is a game, a way to make a living. It isn't as important as his faith and his family.

Now, to some other quarterbacks. Steve Grogan of New England reminds me of me. He has enough ability to take his team all the way, but he's still accumulating knowledge of the game. His team is just about there. I worry about him getting hurt, because he likes to carry the football. But I see nothing but great things ahead for Steve and the Patriots.

When I watched Richard Todd at Alabama, I never dreamed that he would get drafted. But he did, and what he's done has been amazing. And the New York Jets have another good young quarterback in Matt Robinson. They're aggressive and confident. I like both Todd and Robinson.

The guy who backs me up, Mike Kruczek, could be playing regularly on a lot of teams. He's the strongest quarterback in the league, and for as young as he is, he has plenty of poise. He's a wonderful person and a great friend of mine. He doesn't have a great arm, but he has all the other qualities that go into making a top quarterback.

Joe Ferguson of the Buffalo Bills has probably the quickest release in football. He's the best medium-range and short passer I've ever seen. They're rebuilding the Buffalo team, but I predict before Ferguson is through he'll be recognized as one of the best quarterbacks ever to play the game.

If Bert Jones stays healthy, he'll be in the same category. He's cocky. He has a great arm. Great talent, and he's a fiery leader. He's young and eager to get into the Super Bowl and sometimes he comes across as being arrogant and cocksure. But he has a ton of talent.

I've skipped around the league and mentioned some quarterbacks who come to mind quickly. I remember that Dan Fouts of San Diego said he's a better quarterback than I. I don't know him, but I know I could never make statements like that, and I don't see how other people can. What's the point? Why should Fouts, or anyone else, want to compare himself with other quarterbacks? Lots of guys are better than I am—Griese, Staubach, Ferguson, Stabler, Jones, maybe some others. Fouts isn't. Not yet.

As a sportswriter for many years in New York, Detroit, and Pittsburgh, Vito Stellino knows he must try very hard to keep from rooting for a particular team or an athlete. He realizes that by getting too close to the front office or the coaching staff he may wind up being a "homer." By being pals with the athlete he can quickly become a fountain of misinformation and prejudice. He arrived in Pittsburgh to cover the Steeler beat in September 1974—just as Terry Bradshaw was hitting bottom in both his personal and professional life—and as the sides had been clearly drawn in the battle for the quarterback job. It's a controversy he will always remember:

"Gilliam had been given the starting job even though Bradshaw had been the quarterback for four seasons. And there were still a lot of people who wanted Hanratty to be the starting quarterback. The coach wasn't communicating with the media and apparently wasn't saying much to the players either. The club got off all right with a 4-1-1 record even though the defense was doing most of the work. People were grumbling. Gilliam was getting hate mail. Bradshaw was just trying to play it cool. After six games, Noll switched to Bradshaw as the starter. That was also the game when Franco Harris got back into the lineup. The Steelers beat Atlanta, then Terry was in there when they beat Philadelphia, and then they lost to Cincinnati.

"But I don't think anyone could have beaten Cincinnati that day. Kenny Anderson had a phenomenal performance—he was something like 20 for 22, just unbelievable!—and there was no big outcry in Pittsburgh to bench Bradshaw again. But the next Friday, when I arrived at practice, I heard a rumor that Hanratty was going to get the start in the Cleveland game Sunday. I thought it was a joke. Once I spoke with Bradshaw, I realized it wasn't funny at all to him. As it turned out, Noll didn't announce the change to the players until that very morning. He's never adequately explained to this day why he did it. Over the years, Noll has accused the media of fueling this controversy, but the media didn't bring it about: he did. Hanratty didn't have a good game against Cleveland, but you couldn't have expected him to. He literally hadn't played in months. All that did was throw kerosene on the fire.

"So our newspaper conducted a readers' poll on the quarterback situation. In one week we got three-thousand letters! Bradshaw was the winner, although he didn't get more than 50 percent of the votes. It was the number one topic of conversation in Pittsburgh. Once Bradshaw got back in there the following week against New Orleans, there was no getting him out again. And the team went on to win the Super Bowl!

"From my observations, Terry didn't grab hold and take charge of the club with all the authority in the world right from that point. Rather, it was a gradual thing. The confidence came game by game. He grew a beard at about that time. Maybe he was trying to effect some sort of change, or some feeling deep inside about himself. But there was a change that came over him. Even after that, the team was winning on defense and running, but I knew Brad was making important strides as far as the leadership of the team was concerned. And a lot of people forget that he played hurt for the next several years."

(Terry suffered hand and knee injuries in 1975, suffered a concussion and a wrist sprain that kept him out of five games in 1976, and stayed in the lineup in 1977 even after getting a broken wrist in the fourth game of the season against Houston.)

"In 1977 the coach said publicly that Bradshaw was his man, his quarterback. And that's what Brad needed all along. Even if he thought it or felt it, he needed to hear it. And how the boos bothered him! Maybe he liked to let on that he understood and that it was a part of the game, but it pained him terribly. Now the fans don't boo him any more. He's their man too. The fans just love him, but it was a long time happening."

One Answered Prayer

10 One of the difficult things for me to do as a Christian is to pray unselfishly. Let's face it: we pray for specific needs, to ease particular burdens, to get temptation out of our way, to relieve certain tensions and anxieties. We ask God, directly, to heal our sicknesses and to get rid of loneliness and to give us direction. It happens to me, and perhaps this is the experience of other believers as well, that I find myself wanting God to answer Terry Bradshaw's prayers in the manner Terry Bradshaw already has prescribed. I know what I want: I just want God to help me get it.

I know that's not the right thing to do. I know how to pray, and I've never been at all bashful about praying out loud or praying in public. I don't write out my prayers in advance, no matter what kind of audience I'm facing; I simply stand up there and wait upon the Lord and I assume the Spirit will lead me—and that's the way it has always happened. I believe God will give me the right words to say, no matter how tough the situation might be. There's never been a minute of embarrassment in my prayers.

Jesus told His disciples exactly how to pray, and one of the very first things He mentioned was, ". . . *Thy* will be done." Even when He was on His knees in the Garden, He said, ". . . Not my will but Thine." I'm confessing to the world now that sometimes when I pray I'm really hoping that God's will fits right in with mine. Sometimes I'm requesting affirmation of my own beliefs.

A few years ago when things were very bleak and I was bellowing like a sick heifer about my troubles, I specifically prayed each night for God to lead me to a Christian woman— someone who believed in God as I do and who would share my faith and my life with me. I had been divorced, and I was really down. Instead of reaching up to God in those times, I was mired in self-pity. I had read what the Bible said about divorce and so I just quit praying, quit going to church, quit witnessing, and quit just about everything that was decent and wholesome. At that time I firmly believed that I was totally out of fellowship with God and that it was God's choice because of the divorce.

Hollis Haff, a terrific Christian gentleman who is our team chaplain in Pittsburgh, pulled me out of the doldrums. He explained the Bible to me in ways I had never heard it explained before. He taught me things about studying the Word and searching the Scriptures for answers to life's problems. He didn't tell me I had not sinned: I had. He knew it, I knew it, and God surely knew it. But that didn't mean I was right away to be cast into hell for it. Hollis taught me that God not only is *willing* to forgive me, even for that, but is also *eager* to forgive me. Hollis made me understand that God hates sin but loves sinners and that the very reason He sent His Son into the world was to forgive not just Terry Bradshaw, but every person who believes in Him. My relationship with Hollis has been one of the most rewarding experiences of my entire Christian faith. He opened up scriptural doors that I never knew existed.

Once I began an intelligent study of God's Word, I found the answers. This isn't to say that all my problems were immediately behind me and that life was nothing but sunshine and roses. That hasn't been the case at all. In some ways there have been greater trials and tests since I made what I'll call my reinforced commitment to Jesus Christ. But at least now I understand that God puts tribulation on His very own for His own reasons. And I have come to understand what I once read on a little sign: *Sometimes when we think our prayers aren't being answered, they are—but the answer is no.*

Since the turnaround in my life and a new daily fellowship with Christ, I've found that practically every time I read the Bible I come across something that turns a big light on in my life. I'd heard and read things for years, and some things over and over again. But once I was searching in the right way and once I really let God take control of my life, I began to get new insight. I'd heard a thousand times that God stands at the door and knocks and if any man opens that door, God will come into his life (Revelation 3:20). *Now* when I read that passage, I get a special feeling when it says *any* man. That means anyone in the world, no matter what! To me, that means that no matter how deeply we may be in sin, God still loves us and wants to be our friend and our Redeemer. His Son died for the worst, the best, and all those in-between sinners of the world! And when He says that *no* man comes to the Father except through a saving knowledge of Jesus Christ, that spells it out beautifully for me (John 14:6). God really didn't mince words. He spelled it right out that no matter how good we may be, no matter how kind we might be, no matter how many good works we may do, no matter anything—unless we love the Lord and give our lives to Him, there's just no way we can go to heaven.

It took nine years in the National Football League for me to get accepted as a good quarterback. It took me the same number of years to be able to stand up and say publicly that I believe in God and that I want to follow Him. Yet it took me twenty-six years to accept not only the blessings of being a Christian, but the responsibilities that go with being one of God's children. It took me twenty-six years just to begin to understand what it means to really follow Christ, to try to be like Him, to witness for Him, and to make Him the king of my life. For a long time I kept pushing God off the throne of my life and putting Terry Bradshaw up there. I made myself sort of the "designated king," you might say. But that made me a pretender and I've learned that there can be just one King.

Hollis Haff knew of my loneliness. I shot straight from the hip with him and he knew I had been living for myself and not for Jesus. And when I turned things around, I felt from the very beginning that a man's life cannot be really complete and fulfilled without the love of a woman. I knew if I found someone else, it would have to be someone with strong faith.

The situation had changed in my professional life. We had won our first Super Bowl. I felt—or was beginning to feel, anyway—that I could contribute to the team and get the respect of the coaches and my teammates. The Pittsburgh organization had been good to me. I had purchased my ranch in Louisiana. I was getting a pretty good start in the cattle and quarterhorse business.

I had gone to an ice show in Pittsburgh the year before with a couple of my teammates. About the only person whom I noticed in the whole show was a pretty blonde in a green dress. I admitted outright that I wanted to meet her. She was very beautiful. We met some of the skaters after the show, and I forthrightly asked one of them if it would be possible to meet the girl in the green dress. She said, "You mean Jo Jo?" As it turned out, I didn't know who Jo Jo Starbuck was, and she didn't know who Terry Bradshaw was. We met, just briefly, and I asked her if she'd like to go out for a bite to eat. She made some excuse about having some phone calls to make. I found out later she was uncomfortable because there were several of us standing around and it seemed to her we were already paired off.

The following season, after we beat the Vikings in our first trip to the Super Bowl, I tried to reach her, but we couldn't make connections. By the time she was able to return my call, I was on the road and didn't get the message. We were opening the season against San Diego, and I wasn't aware Jo Jo was in town with the east company of Ice Capades. One day a message came through the Steeler office that I was to call Jo Jo Starbuck. For the life of me, I couldn't place her. I asked one of the players, and he said, "Terry, that's the skater in the green dress." I raced to the nearest phone and called her, and after we talked for a bit, she asked if I'd like to come to the show that night. She said she'd leave two tickets if I wanted to bring a friend. I made it a point to tell her I wouldn't be bringing anybody, and invited her to go out after the show.

Jo Jo and I met backstage and later drove out to a place on Route 19 outside Pittsburgh—a pancake house. We sat there and talked till 4:30 in the morning. All we talked about was our Christian beliefs, our faith in God, the direction our lives were taking—or not taking, as the case might be.

It really was a whirlwind experience. It seemed as if God had looked down and saw my needs, and hers, and touched both our lives. Two weeks, maybe three, after our first date, I abruptly asked Jo Jo to marry me. She took a couple of weeks to think it over, then made me the happiest man in the world by telling me yes.

We were married in June 1976.

Both of us quickly learned the real meaning of that old line that marriages may very well be made in heaven, but they have to be lived here on earth.

Fellowship

11 There is an organization called the Fellowship of Christian Athletes, and the person who devised the name should have a street named for him.

It's more than just a catchy phrase. It's one of the wonderful realities of the world of sports. On ABC's "Wide World of Sports," people hear each week about "the thrill of victory and the agony of defeat." We who compete know the real meaning of that.

Once I got my priorities straightened out and learned the true meaning of Christianity, I discovered that there's a great deal of difference in having an interest or even some knowledge about religion and in working toward what St. Paul called "the high calling." We all seek perfection. In sports we seek victory, and if it's an attainable goal, then we have every right to feel terrible when we lose. I hate to hear an announcer say that one team or an athlete has been "humiliated." I cringe when someone writes in the newspaper that some team has been "embarrassed." If you give your best, there should never be any reason to be embarrassed or humiliated even if you get beat 70 to 0. A rout doesn't mean humiliation. If you were beaten by a better team, you still should lift your head high, knowing that you gave every ounce that you had toward victory. If you missed your assignments or failed to execute properly or had your mind somewhere else, it's tough to keep from putting your head in your hands.

When Super Bowl XIII became history, Roger Staubach and I met and shook hands and exchanged congratulations. Neither team had any reason to be ashamed of the effort that afternoon. Now, there was nothing I could say to Roger that would ease the sting of defeat. I couldn't make him feel any better, because he's not only a great competitor but a truly great quarterback. But more than that, he's one of the nicest Christian gentlemen I've ever met. He lives his faith every day and, as much as he wants to win, football isn't the God of his life. I know that when I'm all through with this game—or I should say when it's through with me—I'll treasure the fellowships I've had in this game just as thoroughly as the victories we've had, and that includes those in the Super Bowl.

The Bible tells us to surround ourselves with people of strong faith. By being around Roger Staubach and the many other committed Christians I've met in football, from the high school level up through the professional ranks, I have become a better human being. Way back before I got into the National Football League, there were chapel sessions that drew maybe only two or three players. Now I guess every club has regular chapel services and I'm certain many of them—like the Steelers—have regular weekly Bible study programs. It's one thing to accept Christ as Savior and to make a public declaration, but I think all His children have the obligation to study the Word and learn as much as they can so that they might grow as Christians. Right after the Pro Bowl this past year, a group of athletes attended a Christian conference in Dallas. It was a time for putting the game aside and for getting together with our wives and discussing problems that are unique to pro football players.

We live in an unreal world. There must be unique problems in every business, but professional football has a set of them that can be overwhelming if we're not emotionally and spiritually prepared for them. We're on the road a great deal; there are extended times of separation from wives and children. There are people (like the girls called "groupies" or "camp followers") who like to hang around athletes and who

In the third grade   In junior high school

Overleaf: George S. Gaadt

Lloyd Stilley, The Shreveport Times

Lloyd Stilley, The Shreveport Times

(Above) Terry as a senior and starting quarterback at Woodlawn High School, Shreveport. (Left) Terry watches actor-director Michael Landon hurl the javelin. Both were national javelin champions in their high school days.

Terry looks for a receiver in the 1970 Homecoming game against University of Southern Mississippi. Louisiana Tech suffered its only loss of the regular season that day, 24-23.

Terry set passing and total offense records as quarterback of the Louisiana Tech Bulldogs.

Terry has an emotional moment as Dr. F. Jay Taylor, president of Louisiana Tech University, officially retires famous uniform No. 12 shortly before the 1970 pro football draft.

Louisiana Tech University

Langston McEachern. The Shreveport Times

Dad Bill Bradshaw looks on as Terry gets the news from the Pittsburgh Steelers that he is the number one selection in the pro football draft.

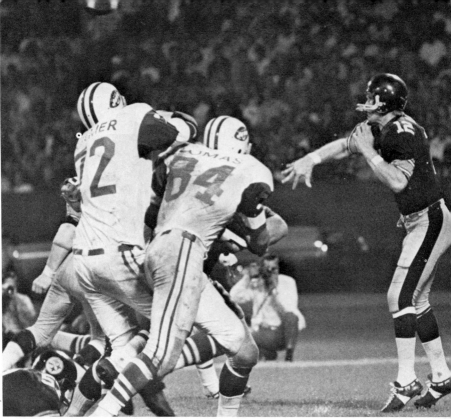

Harry Homa

Harry Homa

(Above) Terry
unleashes a pass
against the New
York Jets in a
pre-season game
in his rookie year
with the Steelers.
(Left) Terry was
often overeager to
run with the ball
early in his pro
career.

Billy Upshaw, The Shreveport Times

Harry Homa

Harry Homa

(Top left) After the 1970 draft, Terry beams
happily with Daniel M. Rooney (left),
president of the Steelers, and Maxie
Lambright, Terry's coach at Louisiana Tech.
(Bottom left) Autograph seekers surround
their hero at his first summer training camp.
(Above) At midfield
in then-unfinished Three Rivers Stadium,
Terry signs his first Steelers
contract as dad Bill Bradshaw (left),
Dan Rooney of the Steelers (second from left),
and Robert Pugh, an attorney.

(Right) Terry scrambles
for a short gain in
Super Bowl X in January 1976, in which
the Steelers defeated the Dallas
Cowboys, 21-17. A year earlier,
Pittsburgh beat the Minnesota Vikings
in Super Bowl IX, 16-6.

Steelers Coach Chuck Noll and Terry have had
many intense sideline discussions. This one
took place in 1971.

Harry Homa

This is Terry battling both the Baltimore Colts and a snowstorm.

It's slippery going, but the outcome is all right as the Steelers overcome the Houston Oilers in the 1978 playoffs en route to Super Bowl XIII.

Harry Homa

Harry Homa

Terry lets the coaches on the sidelines
know how far it is to a first down in
playoff action against the Denver Broncos
in 1978.

Harry Homa

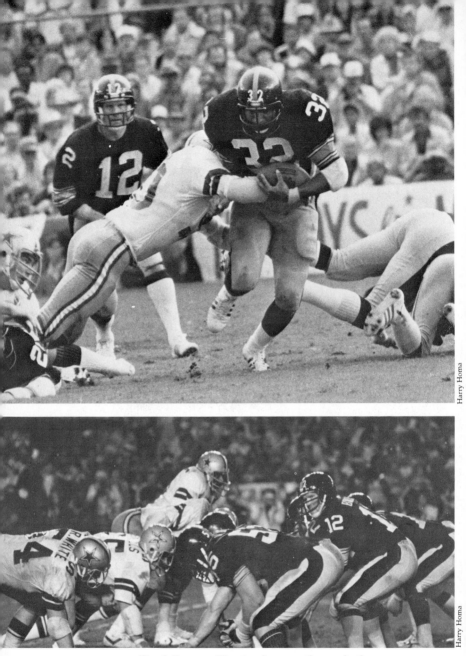

(Top) Franco Harris charges through the middle after a Bradshaw handoff in Super Bowl XIII. (Bottom) Ready for the snap from center in a crucial play against Dallas. Pittsburgh won the Super Bowl game, 35-31.

Harry Homa

Harry Homa

(Top) This billboard was intended to make up
for Terry's being booed during his guest
appearance at a country music concert in his
hometown in February 1979. (Bottom left) Terry
watches the defense from the sidelines. (Bottom
right) Steelers teammate, defensive tackle
"Mean Joe" Greene.

(Top) The Bradshaw family: (from left)
Terry's older brother, Gary; Terry; his
mother, Novis; his father, Bill; his
younger brother, Craig. (Bottom) Jo Jo
Starbuck.

derive some special satisfaction from being with well-known people. Pro football is a pretty closed society, and those on the outside often don't understand its closeness. Millions of young men would like nothing better than to play the game, but only about eleven- or twelve-hundred do it. It's a mighty small segment of the population.

Once a person is into a society and a part of it, he has to have a special understanding of its problems. Sure, there are many opportunities to cheat. Sure, lots of people are telling you how great you are and pumping you up: you're a hero to them because you're doing something they always wanted to do. Perhaps they're living their lives over again through you. Some fathers do that with their kids and end up making life miserable for the youngsters. The point is that it takes a special kind of strength for a guy to keep his head screwed on straight when he's in the public eye; it takes a special kind of understanding for his mate to tolerate some of the problems he will naturally face.

We grow. We grow physically, and it is hoped we grow emotionally and spiritually. As we become more aware of the world we live in, we should change as individuals. Unless we have spiritual growth, we become stagnant Christians, then backsliding Christians, and then if we're not careful we become very un-Christian. On the other hand, some marriages fail because people are continually changing and sometimes don't grow in the same direction.

At our conference in Dallas, we broke up into various groups, determined sometimes by how advanced we are in our Christian studies and sometimes by the problems we face. Some couples who have a strain in their marriage could talk with other couples facing the same obstacles. There were gifted teachers and counselors there to help us along.

Some players there had held their problems inside them because they felt they couldn't share them with their teammates. Maybe they thought the majority of their teammates weren't committed and wouldn't really understand. Maybe they'd think the whole thing was silly. Guys would say, "I'm a Christian, but I'm falling way short of what I know God wants for me, short of what I know in my heart I could be doing as a

Christian." Guys really poured their hearts out, and in many cases the wives did too. All of us were seeking something, wanting to know how we could improve our relationship with God. I think all of us really felt comfortable, felt we could say anything and find some understanding and help for our particular needs. We had various discussion groups with Christian leaders for each group. We could learn how to study the Bible better, how to pray and have fellowship, how to feel better about yourself in the struggle to become a better person, and how to understand and accept our own shortcomings, with the realization that God loves us and understands when we fail.

I really felt the Holy Spirit moving in this group. Everyone was praying for everyone else. All of us sensed God's presence in this get-together. An outsider couldn't really comprehend what goes on inside these sessions. Some players needed help in witnessing: they'd studied the Word and knew they were supposed to witness, but they had trouble opening up. Because of the nature of the game that we all play and the ups and downs that are built into football, other players had special needs in being able to accept the peaks and valleys of the game. If a guy wasn't getting along well with some of his teammates or his coaches, the conference was the place where everybody could open up and benefit from that experience. We may have a problem that we're very reluctant to talk about. Maybe we've kept it bottled up for many months. The minute we get up enough courage to spit it out and talk about it, we find there are a dozen other players who've gone through that same terrible experience. This was a place where that could happen, where Christians really reach out in fellowship and touch each other. I'm sure every person there went away enriched and spiritually nourished.

When I first joined the Pittsburgh team, there was just a handful of guys sharing a common Christian outreach. We could have held our chapel services in a telephone booth. Now we average seventeen or eighteen guys each week. But even in those early years, we learned there were other Christians on the team who were bashful about stepping up and saying, "Hey, I belong in this group. I'm a believer too." In my case, I came to Pittsburgh witnessing. I had spoken openly to the sportswriters and in front of television cameras. People knew I was a Christian. They called me the "Bible-toting quarterback" and things like that.

Then they saw me backsliding. They watched me go up and down the ladder. I didn't go around yelling "Praise God" and handing out tracts and putting notes into my teammates' lockers. I never grabbed anyone by the neck and asked, "Are you right with God?" I guess I was afraid of stepping on someone. My way of sharing was to try to live the good life. Most of the time I did; sometimes I slipped pretty badly. Once in a while another player would come to me and share with me that he is a Christian. When Hollis Haff joined us as our chapel leader, many players felt more comfortable. It was important to have a leader, and he recruited guys into our service in a very quiet, gentle way. Several guys have become saved through the chapel service. Right now, Donnie Shell probably is the ringleader of our club. Donnie's really on fire for the Lord!

We pray a lot for every member of the team. I feel right now there are some tremendous human beings on our club who'd like to join our group, but they just can't seem to take that one step through the door. Maybe they're caught up in something else at the moment—I can well understand that—but I think eventually more of them will come over. There's a lot of spiritual food in those services. We get it from Hollis, and we get it from each other.

Before the last Super Bowl, I made a remark in Miami about my Christian faith and said that God is the central figure in my life and that He should get all the headlines after the game. Don't you know that some guy went on the radio down there and said, "We don't want to hear all that garbage. This is the Super Bowl. Let's keep religion out of it." Well, that's his business if he thinks that way. But I know that the Super Bowl was a great platform for witnessing for the Lord. In the Bible there are many, many stories about people who turned a deaf ear to the teachings of God. Look at the things the apostle Paul accomplished and the writings that we study so much today—yet he had to be struck blind in order to get his life in shape and get things on the right track.

Since I've grown up in my Christian faith, I've done some thinking about what it took to get me to the place where I'm not backsliding and I'm not wishy-washy about it. Maybe that was God's plan. He knew all along, better than I did, how much I could endure. When I gave up on Him, there wasn't a single time He turned His back on me. I have a conscious awareness of Christ now and feel very much saved and extremely happy about it. I'm a happy person inside, no matter what happens in every other relationship in life. I'm confident I can weather any storm. As a child, I knew only a fear of God; I was consumed by His wrath. I still think about it once in a while, and I know God could severely punish me. But the difference is, I know His choice is to save me and to give me the peace "that passes all understanding" (Philippians 4:7). When good things happen to me, I think of the joy I've received from Him and I realize that this is all very temporary and that there is a far greater joy waiting for me.

I keep my Bible with me, and I especially enjoy reading the New Testament. I make it a point each summer when I go to training camp to read the New Testament clear through, even though I've read it many times before—because every time I do, I get new insight. It's a spiritual growth for me. There are mysteries I don't understand, and it's still tough for me to comprehend some parts of the Old Testament. But I'm confident that as I mature as a Christian, God will give me a better understanding as I am able to accept it. He knows how much I can absorb. It's written that when we are children, we think like children and behave like children and speak like children. But there comes a time when we have to put away childish things (1 Corinthians 13:11). Christianity is no toy. Spiritual growth, to me, means the development of the conscience of a Christian. And to me that means knowing God's plan for us, understanding what He would have us do, and taking on more and more responsibility as one of His children. The deeper the commitment I make to Him, the more I surrender to Him, the more I let Him rule my life, then the greater the opportunities and challenges He will present to me. And if along the way He gives me more adversity, I'm positive He'll give me the strength to ride that out too.

In my maturation as a Christian—and I don't mean to leave anyone with the impression that I'm through growing—one of the most difficult things for me to understand has been that God doesn't sit up there and say, "Okay, Terry, you did this nice thing for me and here's your reward right now." I think He counts and measures—it says in the Bible that every hair on our head is numbered and that a sparrow does not fall without Him knowing it (Matthew 10:29-31)—but I don't think any of us has the right to expect payment from God for services rendered. We will get our reward from Him, in His time, according to His schedule, not ours. And, too, we can't become disenchanted because His plan may not dovetail into our schedule. I've read in the Bible that we are not to be weary in well-doing. To me, that means we shouldn't get tired and faint just because we don't see immediate results. On the occasion that I share fellowship with people, mostly athletes, who've just come to a saving knowledge of Jesus Christ, it seems some of them expect radical, overnight changes in themselves. I try to point out a portion of the Word that's been very meaningful to me (Galatians 6:9: "And let us not be weary in well doing: for in due season we shall reap, if we faint not") and helped me through some rough seas when I thought God wasn't responding. He was responding, of course, but not in the way Terry Bradshaw wanted Him to. The only way I learned to accept this was through studying the Word of God and by having sharing experiences with older, wiser Christians, receiving the benefit of their knowledge through fellowship.

It's difficult for young Christians to understand why some people seem to have a great deal of trouble: good people, super Christians. I went through most of my early life as a believer, but was unable to get it through my head why some of God's children suffer so much. Then, through reading the Bible I came to a fuller understanding of what God's plan was for that person and how beautifully that person might have been used, for example, as a Christian witness. Chances are, if God put those heavy crosses on an unsaved person he would collapse under the pressure and nothing good would come out of it. But if a nonbeliever sees a Christian going through some drastic times and being kicked around time after time, yet managing a smile and a kind word and still being strong in the faith, think what meaning that could have in his life!

When we think we have a pile of troubles around us, we should read the Book of Job. Particularly chapter 3. Job was so down and out that he cursed the day he was born. Yet, in the very first chapter, he is described as perfect and upright, a man who feared God and avoided evil. He was called "the greatest of all the men of the east." He had obviously acquired a lot of wealth and had a wonderful family. But everything was taken from him—everything except his belief in God. He lost his family and his worldly possessions; it seemed as if everybody and everything was lined up against him. And all Job really wanted to know was what he had done wrong, what he could do to make things right with God. As a youngster I used to hear older people talking about a particular person and they'd say that he or she "has the patience of Job." I didn't know until I searched the Word that this expression, like many others we commonly use today, comes from the Bible. Today when I feel down and out and think I'm having a bad time, I turn to the Book of Job and I realize that by being faithful servants of the Lord, we can end up like Job—having twice as much as we ever dreamed possible. And that doesn't mean—to me, anyway—that the reward will come to each of us in our lifetimes as it did to Job after all his suffering. But I'm certain of this much: it will come, if not in this life, then in the next.

I have said that the Old Testament is much more difficult for me to understand than the New. But recently, on the recommendation of a preacher friend of mine, I studied the twentieth chapter of Jeremiah. I found that Jeremiah was called to be a prophet and he protested to God that he didn't know how to speak because he was just a child. But God told him he should go and do whatever the Lord commanded, and He promised to tell Jeremiah what to say (Jeremiah 1:6-7). And God did. But in chapter 20 we learn that Jeremiah became so weary that he complained about people mocking him and making fun of him. And like Job, Jeremiah cursed the day he was born and wondered why he had been born to know only "toil and sorrow" and to end his days "in shame." I believe even the stoutest of Christians goes through periods of darkness like that, when he wonders if God is listening to him and if He cares what happens to him. This even happened to Jesus when He was on the cross and cried out in agony that God had forsaken Him.

This is why the fellowship of other Christians is so important to me. When my own strength is not sufficient, I can draw power from Christians around me. I know that every day of my life, whether I'm with my family at my ranch in Louisana, on the road witnessing before some group, or doing my job with the Pittsburgh Steelers, I'm going to be around other Christians from whom I can borrow strength. And more importantly, the Lord is always with me.

Images

12 When I was a youngster growing up in Shreveport, I watched a lot of baseball on television and for some reason adopted the Milwaukee Braves as "my team." They were winners. They seemed to be a tough bunch of players, and I especially liked Joe Adcock. Since then I've gotten to know Joe, who has a farm not too far down the road from my ranch in Grand Cane, Louisiana.

In those days of childhood, I loved to listen to Dizzy Dean do the games on the tube. He seemed to have a lot of fun, and he was forever cracking jokes. He appeared to enjoy life to the fullest and didn't take himself too seriously. Someone once said that Ol' Diz didn't know the meaning of the word "fear," and someone else is supposed to have replied that there were lots of words Diz didn't know the meaning of. Ol' Diz was anything but dumb. He might have been country pure and simple, but he was dumb only like a fox.

My point is that we build certain images of people, and then we discover that those images are not always an accurate description. I had my own image when I made that trip from Louisiana to Pittsburgh, and I quickly found out that what I knew myself to be, way down deep inside, and what people thought I was—well, they were poles apart. The mental picture I had painted of the city of Pittsburgh, the way I figured the veteran players would be, the thoughts I had about rookie camp, the things I'd encounter as I traveled around the National Football League—all these things were images rolling around in my mind.

"Image" is a big word. People pay thousands of dollars to someone to create a certain image for them personally or in behalf of a particular product. Big corporations have public relations staffs to work with images. In these times, almost every outfit you can name—from universities to corporations to rock stars to show business personalities to the guy down the street who thinks he's built a better mousetrap—has a big concern about image. They're concerned about what the general public thinks of them. So am I concerned, but I don't want anyone trying to change what Terry Bradshaw is or how he thinks or what he believes. I guess the old saying "What you see is what you get" fits me to a tee. The times in my life when I've consciously tried to alter what I really am—well, they've always resulted in trouble. At the age of thirty-one, I think I've learned at least this much, that if I can just tend to the business of being myself, then I can cope with about anything that comes up. When I was *talking* more about Jesus Christ than I was trying to *live* like Him, I got into some pretty deep water. When I was trying to be what the *fans* wanted me to be as a quarterback, I wasn't very consistent. When I was trying to please everyone who interviewed me by saying the things I thought they wanted to hear, I wound up confused by my own words and sometimes hurt by what appeared in print or wound up on television and radio.

I'm not much on Shakespeare—I much prefer the stuff Hank Williams wrote—but I remember he said something about "To thine own self be true . . ." and I'll buy that. I got a kick out of the great country singer Willie Nelson's being invited to come to the White House and meet President Carter. Ol' Willie showed up just being Willie: he had his overalls on and that red bandanna around his head and he wore his sneakers, and someone asked him how's come he didn't dress up. Willie said he figured the President wanted to see him just as he was. Mr. Carter got the real thing, Willie being Willie. That's pretty refreshing to me. I don't think Willie was being disrespectful either to President Carter or to the office. Would it really have been Willie Nelson if he'd have gotten all duded up in a tux? Willie has been the same for years, and finally the world got around to discovering him and decided he's all right. He's one of those guys who took twenty years to become an overnight success.

In reality, each player, each coach, every guy in the Pittsburgh organization is the one most responsible for his own image. But the man I guess you'd say is officially in charge of the "image" of the Steelers is Joe Gordon, the director of public relations. I've never kept any secrets from Joe Gordon. He knows Terry Bradshaw. He knows when things are going well for me and when they're not—and I'm not talking only about my on-the-field performances. If you took a poll of football fans around the country, perhaps most of them would think of the Pittsburgh Steelers as a bunch of rowdy, tough-talking guys who take pleasure in beating up on other people once a week from September to December and, it is hoped, on into the month of January. The truth is, the Steelers probably are no tougher or meaner and maybe no stronger physically than any other team in the league. We've managed to bring together a group of athletes who are dedicated to winning. Coach Noll uses the phrase "Whatever it takes" quite a bit, and the players have more or less adopted that. We just go out and do whatever it takes to win. Yes, we are aggressive. Yes, we are physical. Yes, we are tough. But football is an aggressive, physical, tough game. Check the records and you'll find that over the years we've done very well against what we call "finesse teams." The teams that give us the most trouble, on the other hand, are the teams that play the way we do: the Houston Oilers, for example. They are a team much like ours with rugged linemen and very aggressive and mobile linebackers. Offensively, with the addition of Earl Campbell, they play the game quite like we do.

Talk to the media people in Pittsburgh and they may tell you that our coach is evasive and cold and too businesslike. Well, he's not too businesslike for our players. It took me a long time to figure him out, to try to understand his philosophy and his long-range plan for the ball club. Along the way, I had my feelings hurt because he wasn't as warm and outgoing as I wanted him to be. But he was simply being himself. He had played the game under some great coaches and had been an assistant coach, and I'm sure he learned from a lot of people. But when it came time for him to become a head coach, he couldn't copy someone else; he had to be Chuck Noll. And if people don't understand that, that's tough. You gotta like the results and at the same time understand that his main concern isn't that he says all the right things and does all the things that people expect a head coach to do, but that his overall concept of football is sound.

Hey, there were times—lots of them—when I thought I'd never understand the guy. I think he's truly a coaching genius, but there were times when I wanted to choke him. And I'm sure he felt the same way about me.

*T*erry Bradshaw speaks impulsively, shooting from the hip. Chuck Noll measures every word and most always thinks carefully before he speaks.

Terry Bradshaw likes country and western music. Chuck Noll is a symphony devotee.

They have precious little in common, except on the football field.

Chuck Noll first saw Terry Bradshaw when the young quarterback was practicing for the post-season football games after his senior season at Louisiana Tech:

"I watched mostly from the sidelines and had only a brief chance to talk with him. I could tell he was a very talented guy with all the necessary equipment for the game. The Steelers needed help in a lot of areas. We had needs—dramatic ones—and we were looking for quality football players. That was the big thing, and still is. You have to get quality people if you're going to put something together that's going to get the job done. Every year you evaluate your people and try to determine which ones are still willing to pay the price, because there's a price that has to be paid to be good. Someone once said, 'Success is a journey, not a destination.' In those times, the Steelers had a long way to go.

"There was no disagreement about Terry Bradshaw's

being our number one draft choice. He stood out as the quality football player, so much so that we had people talking trade with us right away. They wanted to trade for our choice, and some of them were willing to give us five, six, or even seven players. But most of what was offered was not quality. From the very beginning, we knew he was the quarterback of the future. The ideal situation is to bring in a young quarterback and let him learn by watching other people, by observing, to bring him along slowly. Well, we didn't have that luxury. It was a situation where Terry was thrown into the fire because he was the best we had even though he had a lot to learn.

"When you're thrown into something under circumstances like that, even with such outstanding potential, you're going to make mistakes. You just can't learn all there is to learn in a short amount of time. You cannot be exposed to all there is to be exposed to in a short period of time. So you're going to go in there, and you're going to look great sometimes and you're going to make mistakes and look bad sometimes. Then you get down. And other people get down right along with you.

"So you make changes along the line to try to lift some of the load off the shoulders of a young quarterback. You have to keep reminding yourself that it's a learning experience. And you're saying, 'Here, sit down. Things aren't going well right now. Just sit down for a while and we'll let someone else do it for you.' It's not done with simply the idea of taking him out. There was never any thought of that with Terry. There was never the thought that he couldn't do the job. It was merely a question of when.

"I probably couldn't have handled that situation any differently than I did. We're talking about functioning as an individual. Just as Terry and the other players function as individuals, so do I. I'm going to do things the way I do because I'm me. Another coach might have handled it differently. I'm certain. Maybe another coach would have thrown his arms around Terry and said, 'Hey, I know what you're going through and I understand.' Let's go back to the first year or two. I have to be able to assess a situation for what it really is. The first thing to do is solve the problems that I have. And we had more problems than most teams. Yelling and screaming wasn't going to get the job done. It wasn't a question of trying to push people any further, because most of them were operating pretty much at capacity. It's just that for a lot of them, that wasn't good enough. We simply didn't have enough skills to be winners.

"I was aware of Terry's feelings in those early years. All of us have our problems, and he had his. Everyone should be aware of his responsibilities, not only to his team but to himself; and I think everyone has a certain amount of fear that he cannot or will not get the job done. Some apprehension is very understandable—that doesn't show a lack of poise at all. As a coach, I go in and I'm constantly trying to check my preparation, making certain I'm covering all the bases. I'm asking people to do things they can do, not things they cannot do. But there are mistakes and everybody makes them, and each man—coaches included—is saying, 'I don't want to foul up' and 'If I can only do *my* job.' That's what a team is: a team is the sum of all the people we have, and if everyone does his job and does it well, then the whole thing will piece together. If every man has the feeling that Terry has—his concern about doing his job—that's fine.

"I suppose if we didn't have that apprehension we would be in trouble. Good, alert teams have a certain awareness. Each man has a responsibility to every other man. There's never been any question of Terry's awareness. He's always had great talent and a great desire to excel, but he kept getting in his own way. He was trying to force things, to make things happen; learning not to do that is a gradual, sometimes slow process."

People still talk about a sideline incident some years ago in New York when it was obvious Noll and Bradshaw were screaming at each other. Bradshaw finally yanked himself away from his coach in an uncommon display of independence and rage. The details are somewhat hazy, but the coach remembers that day too:

"It was a pre-season game against the New York Giants in Yankee Stadium. I really don't remember all the details except that I was upset with our entire organization. We didn't play well either offensively or defensively. We had something like five interceptions and couldn't move the ball. I simply lost my cool, that's all. I lost my poise. I felt at the time that if I could say something harshly it might accomplish something. I don't recall precisely what I said but I'm certain it was harsh. Apparently it had a lasting effect if Terry still remembers it that well.

"The learning process is not a smooth thing. No one likes to be told how to do this, how to do that: he sort of has to find out for himself. As a teacher, I can outline certain things for people, but they're the ones who go into the game and experience those things. Sometimes they have to do it many times, over and over, before what I'm trying to get across gets established. It's something that attacks everybody's ego.

"A coach is trying to establish trust. We're always working on trust. Sometimes it's there, and sometimes when things aren't going particularly well, it may not be there. We do things in terms of what is best overall for our football teams, and that's not always what is in the best interest of an individual. I guess what I'm saying is that Terry Bradshaw had to go through all the things he did in order to arrive where he is today. He had to experience all those things for himself.

"Take children. We cannot force them to grow up. We can't live their lives for them. In fact, sometimes an overzealous parent wants to make all the decisions and take the heat off the children. And he ends up inhibiting the growth of the children. Children, when they're growing up, have to be permitted to make the decisions they're capable of making. It's very tough for them sometimes. But if they don't do some decision-making early, when they get out into the world they find they're incapable of making decisions. We can wind up with a thirty-year-old son who's not mature. Maturity is the ability to make decisions.

"In Terry's case, there were occasions when he'd get himself worked up and in such a state because of his worrying, that we'd recognize that and try to help him, either by putting someone else in for a time or by calling some plays for him. We were trying to help him through some difficult times. Now he's through them. He's a mature quarterback. He's reached the point where he can just go out and let the game happen, let all the good ability come out. He can relax and enjoy the game.

"Terry's big and strong and very accurate. He can throw the ball hard, he can throw the ball with touch, he can throw it any way he wants. He's better physically than anyone I've ever seen. And he no longer limits himself by fear, the fear of not doing something right. You know, fear is a terrible thing. I see it more and more in every activity in which I get involved. Let me give you an example:

"One time I took my son and some of his friends to the ocean for some snorkeling. We spent some time in the pool learning how to do it, then we went to the ocean. It was a very sheltered place. But in the minds of those children, 'Jaws' was everywhere. They were scared to death to go into the water. Finally they took to it slowly. They got in and got involved with the sea life and in finding things, collecting things. And they overcame their fear! I had trouble getting them to come out of the water. When we got together for the trip back, the euphoria of these kids was unreal! They were carrying on and jabbering and talking about all the things they had done.

"Suddenly it dawned on me that here we have people who have just conquered their fears. They conquer fear and they're euphoric. This is an experience we have to have. We may not even understand what's happening at the time, but that's part of the educational process. We experience things then later on we find out what it's all about. It then becomes a part of us and we take it for granted. That's pretty much what has happened with Terry Bradshaw. He has conquered a lot of things and now he can take them for granted. They are part of him. This is not to say he will take a casual approach to the game: he will be as serious and as dedicated and work just as hard as ever. But the job will be easier for him, because he's learned to relax and has conquered his fears.

"There had been a great deal of progress and development and maturity with Terry, but I think he finally put things into place in the 1978 season. We talked about the situation a great deal over a long period of time. We talked about it during our pre-season this past year, and Terry had an excellent pre-season. I was trying to say to him, 'You've got the ability. You're prepared. You've had a good pre-season. The whole idea now is to relax. Go in there and have fun and relax and don't get in your own way.' And in our first game of the regular season against Buffalo, he did just that—and I think that was when he started believing totally in himself. It was his turning point.

"I was fortunate in being able to play on a team with Otto Graham, and during my playing career I played against quarterbacks who will be remembered among the greats of all time. In the years I've been in coaching, I've been able to see a lot of others who would have to be considered great. But there's no question in my mind, Terry Bradshaw is the best I've ever seen."

By most members of the Pittsburgh media, Noll is regarded as diffident, cold. Their relationship is more of an armed truce, and one sportswriter said, "We simply ignore him, and he seems to prefer it that way." Noll would like it to be different, but he can no more change to suit the media than he could to accommodate Terry Bradshaw:

"You care what people think. Everybody cares. You'd like to have good press and you'd like to be able to get your ideas across. But that's a tough thing to do. I've found in dealing with members of the press that their goal is an immediate one—it's right now. They want a story. My goal is that football game, to get people together. Our goals often are at cross purposes. Sometimes when I'm trying to convey an idea to someone in the media, that person is only seeking reinforcement of his own thoughts. I do care about my players. I have a great deal of affection for Terry, for all the players. It's not always shown, perhaps. That's one of those things. There's a great feeling you develop with your people, and people on the outside looking in do not always understand that.

"The common experience is the key to football. You start with people who play the game well. Then it's going to boil down to the amount of work and sacrifice you give to the project. It starts in training camp. You learn. You're together. I articulate one thing and what you hear is going to be based on your experience. I'm not going to give you anything new by word. The only way you're going to get something new is to experience it. You can talk all you want, but it doesn't mean much without that common experience. When you have veteran players who have had that common experience over a period of time, you get on the same page, so to speak. That's when you function well as a team.

"It's not necessarily the people with the best talent who win. I run into people who want to measure talent, position for position, down the line, and maybe the most talented people aren't winning. They may win the battle on paper, but not the battle on the field. It's how you function together, how you complement each other. And you have to bring new talent into this blend all the time and get these new people on the same page, functioning as part of the team. You may find you have someone in there who is a burr rather than a cog. Then you have to change people. You have to get people with the talent to win, but more than that with the willingness and selflessness to do the things necessary to get the most out of that talent. If you can do that, you can make winners out of losers."

*B*efore Chuck Noll came to the Steelers, the club had a long-time image as a loser. I'm no psychology major, but believe me it takes a long time to convince a bunch of guys that they can win, that they're not losers. It's a lot like trying to undergo a personality change, I suppose, because in reality that's what a club does. The personality of the club becomes positive, not negative. Its entire way of thinking changes.

I'll bet there are football fans who thought of our owner, Mr. Art Rooney, as a gruff old guy who kept sticking his nose into the coaches' business. But nothing could be further from the truth. This man put not only his money into the organization, but his heart and soul too. I know this: Anyone who works for the Steelers or has been associated with them will tell you it's a class organization. Not once has Mr. Rooney ever told me how to play quarterback, and I firmly believe he's never made a single suggestion to the coach. But he had an image, because he was the owner who'd been around the longest and lost the most.

They call Joe Greene "Mean Joe Greene," but he's anything but mean. Joe's probably the most decent guy I've ever met in football. If we speak of guys putting the team first, last, and always—well, he's the mold they should use for making an unselfish athlete. I don't think Joe really cares if he ever gets his name in the newspaper or mentioned on television, just as long as the team wins. And as for being mean, well, let's just say he has a job to do on the field, and to do that job well he has to be very talented and aggressive. And he's both. That goes back to what the coach and all of us say—whatever it takes. I've known lots of people who will tell you to call them if you ever need anything. Joe Greene's the kind of guy who senses when you need something and gives it to you before you have to ask. He's just beautiful!

There were times when maybe Joe Greene didn't understand the coach. But ask Joe now, and he'll tell you the same thing that I do—that the man is a genius. Coach Noll is intelligent, and his goal is simple: to be the very best. We all know that. We respect him. We believe in him and in each other. We know that as long as he's the head coach we'll be competitive and successful because he won't settle for anything short of that. He will not let the team die of old age. Chuck never says it, but I know it hurts him to have to trade some people or cut some guys or to tell a rookie there's no room for him on the team. That has to be the toughest thing in the world for a coach to do. Perhaps that's why he stays apart from the players and doesn't get too close to them. That would make it hurt more.

We can have all the individual stars we want but football is a team game. Stale as it sounds, we all really do have to all pull in the same direction. It sounds corny, but it works. For many years I worried myself to death about whether Chuck Noll liked me. He doesn't have to tell me nowadays how much he thinks of me: he loves the Steelers and I'm sure he loves all the players. It's not necessary for him to hire an airplane and write it in smoke up in the sky.

Many times people ask me about the violence in professional football and wonder how I can play such a game and still pretend to be a Christian. I'm not pretending. I am a Christian and proud of it, and I'm proud to be a part of professional football. Do you realize how many people would love to play the game and how few people ever get that opportunity?

While reading my Bible one night, I ran across a verse in First Corinthians (10:31) and it says that whatever we do, we're to do all to the glory of God. I believe that means that we are to throw ourselves into our undertakings with full speed and with all the grit and energy and determination we can muster. Most importantly, we are to do all these things for the glory of God and not to glorify ourselves.

If people have their minds already made up that the very act of playing the game of football is a terrible thing, then I have no answer for them because anything I'd say wouldn't mean a whole lot. I know that God gave me a particular talent—and here we could go back to the parable of the talents in Matthew (chapter 13) or to the passage about hiding our lamps under a bushel (chapter 5)—and my talent is to play football. I feel I have to do the very best I can with that talent, all the time remembering that whatever it is, it's a gift from God. No, the violence of the game doesn't bother me, not a bit. It's not a game designed for sissies.

And here we get into the business of the image again. It's amazing to me the image some people seem to have of Jesus Christ. Man, He was no sissy! How could He have done the things He did? How could He have pulled men to him if He'd been anything but a strong, impressive guy? In my mind I see Him as a very bold and forthright and determined human being who knew what He had to do and went out and did it. Sure, there was a gentle quality to Him. He was kind and considerate and compassionate and all those good things.

I love all the wonderful things He did and the miracles He performed. But the most beautiful way I like to think about Him is remembering that He was a human being, that He lived a relatively short period of time, and that He walked around the way we do. He wasn't unapproachable: He was accessible. He went from town to town and was with the people. He had his feelings hurt. He was disappointed. He was scorned and rejected and tormented and tempted and experienced all the things that we have to go through. That's why He understands Terry Bradshaw and everyone else—because He's been there!

When I first started studying the Word, once I had matured to the point where I had an intellectual approach to Christianity rather than strictly an emotional one, I was overwhelmed at the human experiences of Christ. When He went into the Garden to pray, knowing that His destiny was to go to the cross in order that men might be saved, He prayed that the cup pass from Him. He would not have chosen crucifixion, but He understood that it was God's will, not His, and that was the only way to bring about the ultimate will of God. There just was no other way. But He did pray about it. And even when He was on the cross, He thought God had forsaken Him. Isn't that magnificent, that even the Savior of mankind had this quality about Him? He had been betrayed, denied, and crucified and right in the middle of all of it He was left to die, practically alone, and He asked God to forgive those who had done Him in. And I know in my heart that He died for my sins just as much as He did for the sins of those who were with Him on that Good Friday! And God created all of us in His image. Because He wants us to do our best to be like Him.

The Heroes in My Life

13 I'm a hero-worshiper. I admit it, and I don't think it's an unhealthy thing. Every kid needs heroes, and as far as I can see, it doesn't do a person any harm to keep having heroes even as he gets older.

My first hero was Trey Prather. He was the quarterback at Woodlawn High School and he was exactly what I wanted to be. I waited in the wings until Trey graduated so I could get my chance to play. Even though I was playing behind him, I can honestly say I never had an ounce of resentment toward Trey. He was a fine quarterback and a very decent human being who went on to LSU and who later gave his life for his country in Vietnam.

I had another hero in high school—the Woodlawn High coach, Lee Hedges. He was, and still is, an institution around Shreveport. He was a great coach and a gentle person, and I think every kid in Shreveport dreams of playing for him. I had that dream and was lucky enough for it to come true.

My coach with the Steelers, Chuck Noll, is one of my heroes too, even though we've had some slam-bang disagreements and even though it took many years for us to have a close relationship with each other. He doesn't like the same things I do. We don't see each other socially. But we have a great, common bond, and that is football and his philosophy of

151

the game. He's plenty cool. I'd have to say he's the one who taught me how to study the game of football. He taught me the fine points of the game.

Hollis Haff is another hero of mine. As the team chaplain of the Steelers, he puts everyone else's needs ahead of his own. He sets up our chapel programs and Bible study groups and provides individual counseling when we need it. He's warm, friendly, and understanding. I think Hollis is a perfect example of what a Christian should be. He's had a mighty effect on the lives of some of our players.

Take Ernie Holmes, for example. Some of the problems Ernie had got a lot of publicity. I never really knew how to take him. I couldn't tell whether he was kidding or not. He seemed to be two people, blowing hot and cold. Many people were afraid of him because they never knew when he would fly off the handle. He'd be very uncooperative, then he'd turn it around and be as nice as pie. But Hollis Haff touched Ernie's life and helped him to realize his potential through the Lord. Today Ernie's a beautiful Christian man. Maybe if everyone in the world could see what Christ did in the life of Ernie Holmes, a lot more people would come to know Him.

Hollis is a guy you can level with and you know it'll never leave the room. He's able to gain the confidence of people and help them to recognize their problems and get ahold of them. Hollis will stay right with them—baby-sit them if need be.

Occasionally we read of a well-known athlete who has a problem—maybe gets arrested for something. We don't know what happened, what went wrong. But something did. What a tragedy that is!

Kids look up to football players. I know some kids look up to Terry Bradshaw, and I want always to be worthy of that trust. Some disagree with me, but I strongly believe that people in the public eye have a greater obligation to do and say the right thing. After all, the public put us up there in a manner of speaking. I know talent is what gets us there—but talent without the opportunity to use it doesn't mean a whole lot. If you believe in the parable of the talents—and you have to if you're a follower of the Lord—then you must believe that if more is given to you, the more you owe; the more you have to share; the more you have to give. And I think we should be examples for good for the young people. Sure, we make mistakes—lots of them.

I had a hero when I was in elementary school. A certain guy was very influential in leading me to the Lord. I mean, he was a super Christian. Then some years later I found out he was involved in something pretty shady and wound up doing some time in prison for it. I couldn't believe it! It just floored me! I know how crushed I was when I found out about this person I had trusted and believed in, so I think I can understand how a young person feels today when someone he's idolized messes up. This guy wrote me from prison, and it was hard for me to face him when we finally met again. I wanted to say something meaningful, something to let him know that his life mattered to me, but words failed me. He told me he had prayed about it and had asked God to forgive him, and he seemed to be getting his life on the right track again. But a part of me was destroyed because I had such faith in him and because he'd been such a vital factor in my decision to come forward and accept Jesus Christ as my Lord and Savior.

We find out sometimes that our heroes are tarnished and that, like, everyone else, they sin and come short of the glory of God. All I know for sure is that if some tarnished hero has repented and is truly sorry for what he did, and he asks God to forgive him, God will do just that, just as he's forgiven Terry Bradshaw and thousands of other sinners of the world.

If you're brought up in a Christian home as I was, then your parents are heroes too. My mother and dad and my two brothers are all great Christians, and they've been a great influence for good in my life.

And everyone has a favorite uncle. Mine's my Uncle Bobby Gay, my mom's brother. He believes in working hard and praying hard. He's true blue, that's all. He helps me out on my ranch, he and my Aunt Margie. You just can't find better people on the face of the earth. Bobby's got those basic, true ideas and principles that so many people miss in life these days. All Bobby wants to do is go out and work hard, then come home to his family—I guess we're a lot alike. Sometimes I don't even think of him as my uncle—he's more a friend than anything else. We're together a lot down here on the ranch and we're able to get out alone together and forget all our troubles and cares. We talk about cows and horses, we have a chew, and we dream. We get on top of haystacks and we dream our dreams. We know some of them are wild and won't ever come true, but they're our dreams and nobody can take 'em from us. Bobby's really a true friend and, you might say, a hero of mine. He puts no pressure on me to do anything down here. He can run the place all by himself, and it's four-hundred acres with a hundred head of cattle and twenty-five horses and a lot of work to be done. He's just the best.

Then there's my dad. I've heard people say, "Well, you have to respect so and so because after all he *is* my father." I don't believe that. Respect has to be earned—there's nothing automatic about it. Most anyone can father a child, but that's not the same as being a father and being the person that a father should be.

My dad is my number one hero. He had to grow up fast, and he did without the kind of home life he wanted. When he should have been having fun, he was out scratching out a living. But it gave him a toughness, a determination to provide a good life for his family, and moreover, to see to it there was strong family unity. The Bradshaws have togetherness. My dad, Bill, has always put his family before everything else. When things got toughest for me, I knew I could count on him to listen and understand and give me the right kind of advice so I could make the right decisions. These days we're together all the time, and every day I have more and more love and respect for him. I know he's proud of me, but he couldn't be more proud of me than I am of him.

I have a couple of football heroes, too. Bob Griese is my hero because he's a fine quarterback, mechanically, and he's a thinking quarterback. He never seems to lose his poise. And Roger Staubach embodies all the things I like in a man. He's a dynamic individual, with great talent on the field and a whole lot of competitive fire. But Roger is the total human being, because the Lord is number one in his life. And he's totally wrapped up in his beautiful wife and five children. He's a man who has all his ducks in a row.

And I have to admire his coach. Tom Landry is another of those poised individuals. I can look at him and know that down deep, he has his life in order. One of his former players said he was a "plastic man," but maybe that player didn't have his life together the way Coach Landry does. Tom Landry's a Christian and a man whose life is a strong witness for the Lord. Maybe the world would be a better place if every person were as plastic as Tom Landry!

The guys I play with on the Steelers are all heroes of mine—and that's not just something you yank out of your hat to put in a book. There's no popularity contest on our team. There's not a better runner in the game than Franco Harris, and at the same time he's a totally unselfish individual. We really do have the team concept, and I think that has more to do with our winning than does our talent. There's not a bad guy on our team. Maybe that explains why we've been to the Super Bowl three times and come home a winner every time.

$\mathcal{T}$ here is a saying among public relations people that they're "last to know, first to go."

In sports, particularly at the professional level, the public relations man is in a difficult if not impossible situation. It's at the very least a no-win situation. He is supposed to generate good publicity even for a mediocre team. He is the buffer between the media and the front office, between the players and the public, between the front office and the public, and quite often between the players and the coaches and front office. He's everyone's image-maker or image-changer. He gets the gaff when the coach is uncooperative and uncommunicative. He gets the blame when a player forgets to show up at a Rotary luncheon. He is ignored when things go well.

Perhaps Joe Gordon, the Steelers' director of public relations, has as good a handle as anyone on Terry Bradshaw: "Let's go back to 1969 when Terry Hanratty came to the Steelers. He had been a number two draft choice; there had been a great clamor to draft him. He was relatively local, coming from Butler, Pennsylvania, only thirty miles north of Pittsburgh. He was from Notre Dame, and Pittsburgh probably has as loyal a Notre Dame following as any city in the country. Moreover, Hanratty is half-Italian and he's Catholic, and Pittsburgh has a greater percentage of Italians than any other single ethnic group. So Hanratty had everything going for him.

"Now, here comes Terry Bradshaw the following year. He's the first player chosen in the entire draft and he's the exact opposite from Hanratty. Hanratty has black hair and dark features. He's very smooth, sophisticated, articulate. He's been exposed to the pressures of big-time football at Notre Dame. He's been through the interview mill a hundred times. Here comes Bradshaw, and he talks a little bit differently than we do. He's blond and blue-eyed, and immediately he's regarded as something of an alien or a foreigner. And while Hanratty thinks before he answers, Bradshaw responds impulsively. He's anxious to please and he says whatever comes into his mind. Hanratty thinks before responding; Bradshaw just blurts it right out. The lines are drawn almost immediately: there's a Hanratty faction and a Bradshaw faction.

"Curiously, the two of them got along great and still do. I think each has always respected the fine qualities in the other. I don't think they ever looked upon each other as competition. I think they helped each other, and there's still a strong relationship there. Brad had all the physical equipment and none of the confidence. Hanratty would be the first to tell you that he had the confidence and not nearly so much ability as Brad. Even today, Hanratty will call from his home out in Colorado and talk for a long time over the phone about a game he's seen us play on television, and he marvels at Brad's abilities. No, there's no jealousy there.

"You know the thing that's impressed me as much as anything about Brad, though, is that win or lose, he doesn't duck anyone. He'll come into the dressing room after not having had a particularly good day, and if the team has won he's just excited all over and happy as can be. On the other hand, he's terribly down if we lose, no matter how good an individual day he might have had. And win or lose, he never dodges the press and never ducks a question. He'll stay around the locker for hours, as he did when we lost to Oakland in 1976 in the AFC championship game. Terry just stands there and handles everything. At times it's been very tough for him. I've seen other players duck out or make a quick exit or hide in the trainer's room or take a long time in the shower, but this just isn't Terry Bradshaw's way. He has a lot of courage, both physical and mental. He's incredible!

"Over the years that Terry's been with the club, there haven't been more than three or four times when he's begged off an interview. And he's barraged with requests for them all the time. He's very aware of my function, that it's my job to channel these things to him, and he never growls or snaps at me. Instead he has gone out of his way to accommodate people out of consideration for the club. He's fantastically cooperative. In the early years he wasn't comfortable with the public, and he was very uneasy and sometimes guarded in his comments. That's because he's such a sensitive person. He got to the point—after he'd been through the mill and had his feelings hurt—where he'd weigh every word. Now he just speaks from the heart. He's totally candid.

"It took him a long time to win the fans over. I don't think he totally won them over until the 1978 season. It was a very gradual thing. When we won our first two Super Bowl games, we were primarily a defensive team—we lived or died with our defense. On offense we were very conservative and very much run-oriented. People were reluctant to give Bradshaw the credit he deserved. They'd say anybody can hand the ball off to Franco Harris and all Terry had to do was keep from making mistakes and the defense would come in and give him fairly good field position. So the emphasis was 'Don't make the big mistake. Don't turn the ball over. Just play to our strategy.' In 1977, we changed our offensive philosophy and started throwing the ball more. That's because for the first time during an entire season, our wide receivers were healthy. For the first time in Brad's career he had a true threat at tight end in Benny Cunningham and he had the opportunity to pick his receivers and be a little more selective in where he threw the ball. It was the first year in Chuck Noll's entire regime that we gained more yards throwing the ball than we did running it.

"Terry really loves the game. I've never seen a better-conditioned athlete or a player who is more into the game than he is. We've all heard the old cliché about the guy who'd play the game for nothing. I'm not going to say that about any athlete, because when you reach the age of thirty you're not going to do much of anything for nothing. But if that were ever to be true of anyone, it'd be true of Terry Bradshaw. He comes early, stays late, hangs around the office. It's not a nine-to-five thing with him. He thoroughly enjoys practicing. He enjoys sitting in front of his locker, kibitzing with the other players. He likes the stadium. He'll shag punts if the punter happens to be practicing a lot that day. If there's a spot open, he'll go catch passes—and I really think he could make it as a receiver or as a punter. On Saturdays, which is special teams day, he has to do very little, but he and Mike Kruczek will just punt back and forth with each other across the field. And Terry will consistently punt the ball fifty or fifty-five yards with great accuracy.

"Every year we have a softball game here in the stadium, and I've seen him hit a softball that bounced over the fence on one hop. And it's 335 feet down the line in Three Rivers Stadium! Without the slightest exaggeration, I think he's the kind of guy who would excel at anything, at any position. I think he could make it as a tight end, a linebacker, you name it. Even as a runner.

"But he's even greater as a person. He'll talk with you about his personal life and his beliefs and about yours. He's inquisitive, very interested in people and how they think and what they think of him. There's no doubt about it, what you see is what you get with Terry Bradshaw. Over the years that I've been with three professional sports—basketball, hockey, and football—the only athletes I've ever known who consistently placed the team above their own individual accomplishments are Joe Greene, Jack Ham, Franco Harris, and Terry Bradshaw. I mean, they do it all the time, every day of their lives.

"Some years back, I guess a lot of people thought Terry Bradshaw was wearing his religion on his sleeve and talking about it a great deal and perhaps not living it as well as he talked it. Now he's talking about it less but living it profoundly. He's a great example for good for everyone whose life he touches. He's just a beautiful person."

The Other Bradshaw

14 If there's one thing I know for certain about myself, it is that I can't stand arguments and contention. Life is too precious a gift to waste fighting and holding grudges. It pains me very much to this day that relations between the Bradshaw family and Louisiana Tech University aren't what they should be.

Things couldn't have been better for me when I was there. I had no trouble with anybody, and I think I left there with a lot of good friends that I'll have for the rest of my life. That all changed when my younger brother Craig decided to go to school at Tech. I was against it from the start, and it's not one of those I-told-you-so things either.

Craig played his high school ball at Southwood High, and I guess he could have gone to college at a number of places. But he chose Tech. I told him I didn't think it was a good idea and I explained why: It was inevitable that he'd be compared with me. Not that I was any great shakes, but I am the only one over there to have his jersey retired. There is, or there was, anyway, a life-sized portrait of me hanging over there. My whole presence is there. And for him to go over there as Terry Bradshaw's younger brother—well, it just didn't seem to be a wise thing to do. Now, he could throw the football. He wasn't the most coordinated kid on the field, but he had the gun. He could

159

really fire it, and I'm sure he could throw the ball at 18 or so better than I could at that stage of my career.

In my heart, I am convinced Craig went to Tech to prove to everybody in the world that he wasn't afraid of the challenge. You know 'You gotta face challenges in your life' and all that, and Craig was bound and determined he was gonna go over there and prove to everyone he could handle the pressure of being Terry Bradshaw's younger brother. He didn't expect to play much his freshman year, and he didn't. No problem. I think the problems started in his sophomore year. He wanted to play, but they played another guy ahead of him, and Craig was unhappy.

(The other guy was Keith Thibodeaux, another sophomore, who was named to the all-Southland Conference team. As a sophomore, Craig Bradshaw got into eight games, completed 12 of 35 passes for 143 yards and 0 touchdowns and 1 interception. The team record was 8-1-2.)

I'm in Pittsburgh during this time, and I'm getting telephone calls and he's telling me how unhappy he is and what's happening in practice. I don't want to go into a lot of details, because I'm hearing all this strictly from my brother, and blood is thicker than water and I care only about what is best for him. He said he was being embarrassed in front of his teammates and he felt he didn't have the respect of the coaches. Craig needed a lot of coaching. They knew that over there; I had talked with them about it. I told them, 'You stay with this kid and work with him and work and work and work and he'll be a great one.' Evidently there developed a personality conflict between Craig and one of the coaches. Strangely enough, it was the coach who had been so close and meant so much to me, Mickey Slaughter. Craig didn't like Mickey, and he didn't feel Mickey liked him.

Then I'd get another call, and Craig would be all fired up and tell me he had a long talk with Mickey and everything was gonna be all right. Craig would have a whole different attitude, and then it wouldn't be any time at all and he'd call me again and tell me the bottom had dropped out. Now, I have to say that maybe Craig didn't have the same intensity about football that I've had. Nevertheless, it was messing up his life.

It was getting to the point where he was thoroughly mixed up. He said he had made up his mind, once and for all, that he wanted to leave Tech. He asked me if I could help him get another scholarship somewhere else.

Football can't be your God. Only God should be your God. Football in itself just isn't that important to let it destroy your life. You can't go through life being unhappy, and the fact is, Craig was unhappy at Louisiana Tech, for whatever the reasons and regardless of who was to blame. So I talked to some people and they put me in touch with a person at Utah State. Craig quit Tech and went to Utah State, and he's made a good adjustment and he's very happy. And that's the bottom line. That's the only thing that really matters in this whole deal. But in the meantime, someone over at Tech circulated word that I was the one who persuaded Craig to leave. That's just not true. And I emphasize that I heard only one side of the story, and maybe there are fifteen sides to it.

I'm really sorry that there's some tension now involving my family and Tech. That's my school. I love it, I really do. The people at Tech and the people in Ruston were tremendously nice to me and I'll never forget them for it. But later on, I realized the realities of college athletics. It's a must-win situation. The more you win, the more friends you have. If you produce for a college coach, he gets close to you and that's the way the old ball bounces. If I hadn't been successful over there, if we hadn't won, I have to think that maybe Mickey Slaughter and I wouldn't have been as close. That's only natural.

If Craig hadn't gone there, all this tension could have been avoided. There was just no way it could work out. But no matter what has happened, I have no animosity toward anyone and I'll always love my school and the people over there. What I did, I did for my brother because I love him. And he's happy now. He has a final year of eligibility and maybe he won't play much, because the quarterback who started last year is coming back. But Craig says he's working hard because he wants to get drafted by the pros; he doesn't call me and complain these days. That's all I know about the situation. I'm sure there are other sides to it.

*T*here are. Mickey Slaughter's side goes this way:

"It pains me a great deal even to talk about it. I'm really sorry that Craig didn't work out at Tech. If you look at it from a realistic point of view, nothing would have been more advantageous for Louisiana Tech University than to have another Bradshaw be the number one quarterback. It would have been great for him, for the school, the fans—well, for everyone. But it didn't turn out that way. It happened that he was beaten out. Some say it's my fault; others say it's Craig's fault; others say he was a victim of circumstances. I only know how I view the situation.

"When the waters started getting a little rough, I called Terry in Pittsburgh and informed him of exactly what had happened insofar as his brother was concerned. I told him as honestly as I possibly could what I thought about his brother as a quarterback and, believe me, I didn't pull any punches. I told Terry that Craig was not Terry and never would be in a million years. There's only one Terry. A guy like Terry comes along once in a lifetime. He's a coach's dream. All right, Craig has to be Craig. He's a young man with a lot of interests other than football. He's a fine young man, but he had outside interests. Terry didn't: his all-consuming passion was football. He desperately wanted to succeed and would make any sacrifice to that end. Craig wouldn't. The brothers are different in temperament. But the major difference is in talent. Terry has a tremendous amount, an almost unbelievable amount of God-given ability. Craig has some ability, for sure, but in no way can he ever measure up to Terry. And I told all those things to Terry on the phone. The conversation was pleasant, very warm. I thought at the time we parted with a mutual understanding. But then the boys' father injected himself into the picture, and therein lies the trouble. His dad is angry with Tech, and I don't know what anyone can do about it. He feels Craig didn't get fair treatment, and nothing could be further from the truth.

"I'll say one more thing: You can talk all you want about what Terry has done for the school, but the school did a lot for him too. For all practical purposes, it seems Terry has severed his relationship with the university and that's a great tragedy.

The people down here in Ruston really care. And they didn't desert Terry when Joe Gilliam beat him out for the quarterbacking job with the Steelers, and they didn't turn their backs on him when things weren't going so well. Sure, he's a great football player, but folks in these parts care about him first as a person."

The old coach, Maxie Lambright, doesn't even want to talk about the controversy.

"There was only one Terry Bradshaw," he said. "The thing with his brother just didn't work out. I'm not putting the blame anywhere, but the main problem over all the others is that Craig didn't have nearly the talent to be Terry, and he wasn't good enough to start for our team. It's really as simple as that."

Not quite, if you listen to Bill Bradshaw:

"I'm the guy who didn't want Terry to go to Louisiana Tech and I'm the guy who didn't want Craig to go there—but for different reasons. I'm like every other proud father. I thought Terry should have gone to Baylor, but once he made up his mind it was Tech, I was all for him and for the school, and as it turned out it was a smart thing. But I didn't want Craig to go to Tech for the same reasons Terry didn't want him to go there: people would forever be comparing the two.

"Yet Craig never tried to be Terry. All he wanted to be was Craig Bradshaw, but I think some people expected too much of him. Some folks got on him because he was Terry's kid brother. I made it a point to talk with the coaches after the spring game of his sophomore season. They said it took time for him to fit into their system, but they said they had plans for him and were counting on him, and they said he'd play.

"Well, he didn't play enough to suit him. And he felt he was made to be the goat in scrimmages. He felt the coaches were screaming just at him. He tried to maintain his cool, but he felt he'd never really play much. He did start one game, here at State Fair Stadium in Shreveport, and he didn't do well. About mid-season, I talked with Coach Slaughter and he told me I was talking to the wrong coach—that I should talk to

Coach Lambright. I did, and he told me Craig still fit into their plans and that it would just take time to work his way in. Then Tech recruited another quarterback after that season, and everyone was putting out the word that this young quarterback would give Craig a lot of competition for the backup quarterback's job. That was too much for Craig, and he made up his mind to leave. He wasn't happy, and that's all that mattered to me. I take full responsibility for his leaving. Lots of people thought it was Terry's doing, but between Craig and me, we made the decision that he'd be better off to leave.

"The Bradshaws don't look back. We always look forward and make the best out of whatever comes. Coach Lambright proved over the years he's an outstanding coach, and I personally think Coach Slaughter is an excellent coach. I'm sorry both of them have quit at Tech. Coach Slaughter may not deal with people on a one-to-one basis as well as some do, but he knows his football and he's a fine man. Whatever differences of opinion there might have been, I'd like to think everything is smoothed out now, or at least it can be straightened around. I don't have any bad feelings for anyone. Why, not long ago I had dinner with some of the Tech people and I told 'em I'd do anything in the world for 'em. I told 'em I'd help recruit if they asked. Louisiana Tech is very close to the hearts of all the Bradshaws. Anyway, the Bible teaches us that it's wrong to harbor any grudges and carry around ill will. Besides—as Terry said—the only issue that means anything at all is Craig's happiness. He's happy now. And so are the rest of us."

The Courage to Quit

15 All my football dreams have been fulfilled. I couldn't ask for anything more out of the game, and I've received far more from it than I deserve. All I hope now is that I will know when it's time to walk away.

What I dreamed of as a kid was the chance to play. If we can compare this game to the childhood game of "King of the Mountain," then I thought I had climbed to the top when I became the starting quarterback for Lee Hedges at Woodlawn High School. College was another mountain, and although I went to a smaller school, I received a lot of recognition and from that the opportunity to play with the best players in the world in the National Football League. The fact that our team has done very well is more than anyone had the right to hope for. This isn't to say that we Steelers don't have more goals ahead of us. We have an organization that won't let the team grow old, and there's no reason in the world why we can't continue with the success we've all enjoyed.

Despite all the ups and downs in my career, it's still hard sometimes for me to realize that the 1979 season is my tenth year in professional football. And I'm only thirty-one! Right now I feel as if I'd like to play eight more seasons. That's if I stay healthy. During the past off-season, I had a little repair work done on my left wrist and on my right elbow—nothing dramatic or serious, but just to fix some of the bumps and bruises I've acquired along the way. The Lord blessed me with a pretty sturdy frame, and now that I've developed a skin that's reasonably tough, I don't see any reason why I couldn't play until I'm thirty-eight. I firmly believe a person should consider his body a gift from God and shouldn't do anything to abuse it. I've always been a strong advocate of good conditioning, and I think that's why I've been able to bounce back pretty well from the aches and pains I've had in football.

One time in Pittsburgh, after we won the Super Bowl for the first time, I was honored by the Dapper Dan Club, an organization that does a lot of fine work. Instead of getting up and merely thanking them for the award, I talked about my family and my faith in God. I don't think I said anything to really rile 'em up, but I thought it was as good a time as any to tell the people that I understood that the relationship between the fans and a quarterback is a love-hate thing. That's just the way it is, and every quarterback must understand that. But it took this ol' country boy a bit longer to come around to that way of thinking. I told 'em I knew they loved me at that time but that if I fouled up the next season, I'd catch it from 'em. That's the nature of the game and the nature of my position. One more thing—I also told 'em, "I'm not as dumb as y'all think I am."

The best thing I can do for the Steelers and for myself is to be the first to know when it's time to quit. The first contract I signed was for five years, and then in '74, when things were going to pieces for me, there was all that talk about the World Football League. Some of the players were jumping to the new league. I was ready to listen to anything from anybody at that stage of my career. And I was offered $600,000 over a three-year period, plus a huge bonus for signing. And that was a whole lot more than I was making with Pittsburgh. So I flew to New York to meet with the people from the World Football League. All I wanted was the chance to play for the Steelers, but that was not happening. And I was not going to use the new league as a lever to pry more money out of the Steelers. Playing—not money—was my main objective.

But Dan Rooney knew where my head was. The Rooneys

always know, because they really care so very much about their players. Dan called me up and then flew down here to my ranch and spent a couple of days with me. I laid it right out to him. I told him I didn't understand Chuck Noll, couldn't relate to him, couldn't work for him. At least, at the time I didn't think I could. I told Dan I wasn't getting any support and encouragement from Chuck. Maybe I'm one who needs constant reassurance. There's no maybe involved—I know I'm that way. I know what my own needs are. My confidence was shot; I had trouble with Chuck and trouble with the fans.

About all Dan Rooney did was listen. We sat around the house and talked. We walked around the ranch and I told him about my plans for the place, what I wanted to do with the ranch down the road. He was just a good, decent human being, that's all. He didn't rush down there with a new contract in his pocket, and he didn't try to con me about anything. I don't know if he took what I said back to Pittsburgh and related it to Chuck, but I suppose he might have. I know that when I got back to Pittsburgh, we sat down with the Rooneys and they told me they wanted to extend my contract.

I signed it, because I believed in the organization and because the new deal gave me not only some security, but some awareness that the club really did believe in me and wanted me to remain a part of it. Over the years—I signed another multi-year contract after that—the organization has been very decent with me. I don't run around checking into what other people get paid, and I'm sure there are a lot of quarterbacks and running backs who make much more than I do. I just know the Rooneys are fair, and they've been pleasant to deal with. Even though you may lock horns with them on a certain part of your contract, they've always been able to separate the business dealings from the personal part of their relationship with you.

I've never been jealous of another player's salary. Some people tried to get me to say something bad about the money Joe Namath got, but I say, "Hey, he was a very special athlete and his was a very special case. He came in at a very important time in the history of professional football and he deserved every penny he got." Look at Arnold Palmer in golf! Every golfer out there on tour today should get down on his knees each night and thank God for Arnold Palmer. It was Palmer who made it possible for the golfers to be playing for such high stakes today. And they ought to get on their knees, anyway, just to thank God for their special talents.

But all of us in sports have to realize that the skills diminish, the talents get rusty. It's all gonna be over someday. An injury could wipe it all out tomorrow. And if you're the type of individual who's made football your god, then you're in for a rude shock. People like that will be running around in circles, not knowing what to do with their lives. As much as I love football, I have honestly tried to keep it in a proper framework. I've been playing the game for as long as I can remember, and right now the game is still a lot of fun for me. I enjoy training camp. I enjoy working out. I like the games, the confrontations, the duel that goes on out there on the field. Sure, I get paid for it, but it's fun and it's interesting for me. It's like getting ready for a big battle, then going out and doing it. It's a tremendous challenge.

The question is, What happens to Terry Bradshaw when all that is over? Well, I honestly believe I'll be able to handle it. My family and my ranch mean a great deal to me. I'd be just as happy if I never had to leave the ranch. No, I don't want to divorce myself completely from football. I want to play as long as I can do it effectively. I hated to embarrass my teammates when I was a young quarterback in this league, and I sure don't want to embarrass them—or myself—when I get creaky and old. As Kenny Rogers says in that song, "You gotta know when to hold 'em, / Know when to fold 'em." I know there won't be the big side deals, the speeches, the endorsements. Everyone likes a winner and hardly anyone cares about a loser. They don't even care if you *used* to be a winner. It's now that counts. This is a today society, a today world. And football is an ego trip, no question about that. I want to be financially independent, but even after I get to that point I don't want to just sit around. I want to lead an active, productive life and be of service to others whenever I can.

Some players have knocked the game. I'll never do that. Some players have said the game is dehumanizing. Well, I don't feel as if the game has done that to me. Maybe it's a lack of maturity on the part of the one who feels dehumanized. Football is a demanding occupation that requires a great deal of time. It is also a team game, and to mold an effective team you have to forget a lot of individual considerations and create an atmosphere where the team is your number one concern. It takes drills and lots of studying and a lot of repetition, and you're having someone else's philosophy put on you—but if you can accustom yourself to that and grab ahold of the fact that this is the only way it will work, then I don't think you get robbed of anything. There's nothing dehumanizing about having an eleven o'clock curfew. Everybody in the world ought to be in bed by eleven o'clock anyway.

As much as I look forward to going to camp in the summer, it becomes drudgery. It gets boring. We're there six or seven weeks and it gets tough. When we break camp, it feels as if we're getting out of prison. But we've been there for a purpose, to prepare ourselves mentally and physically for something very important.

Once the season starts, there's another routine. On a normal week, we have Monday off and sometimes I'll go to the stadium for some treatment if I need it, or I'll just hang around and chew the fat with some of the guys, or maybe I'll play golf if the weather is good, or maybe I'll drive over to Atwater, Ohio, and see Bobby Dean Moore, a good buddy of mine who's in the cattle business.

On Tuesday it's back to work. We go over the film of the previous game. We watch it with the coaches, and I look closely to see how I called the game. I want to know why I did that, or didn't do the other thing. I sometimes pretend there's somebody else calling the game and I'm watching to see how he did it. I get to see the coverages again and the play I called. There are things I pick up in film that are really valuable to me, not only for the next time we play that team again but in my overall concept of myself as a quarterback. And the conversations I have with the coaches are vital. It's part of the continuous learning process. Then we run for a while.

Wednesday's a full day. I get to the stadium before nine in the morning, and we have meetings where we learn everything we can about the opposing team's defense. We discuss the opponent's personnel, its "tendencies." I get a complete profile on their defense. Then we get to our game plan. It's prepared by the coaches and we go over it play by play. We're talking here about what we call keys: what we want to do, and when, and the adjustments; the ifs and whys of the whole thing. It's an all-day affair. At home at night I go over the plan and study it and look at more films.

The next day it's more of the same. We are so heavily involved in study and preparation, the average fan wouldn't believe it. We practice in the afternoon for a couple of hours, then after we catch a shower, the quarterbacks have another meeting for about an hour. Usually by Thursday night I have things pretty much down pat in my mind.

Friday is a short day. We practice goal-line and short-yardage situations, scoring-territory plays. We review some basics and try to let the players get their legs back. The soreness from last week's game is pretty much out by then.

On Saturday, we go over the kicking game and loosen up. It's a short day for us. Mike Kruczek and I always have our punting contest on Saturdays. I'm terrific in practice, but I really fouled things up when I had to punt in an actual game.

On Sunday—or sometimes on a Monday night—we put it on the line again. Generally I don't sleep very well the night before a game. And I never can eat the day of a game.

A Monday night TV game is special, no doubt about it. We're more aware on those nights that we're a part of show business, that it's an entertainment thing. It becomes a happening and guys kid around about it. It just carries with it a special feeling that's difficult to put into words.

Now, I'm not suggesting that, when all this day-to-day drama is over for me, the transition will be easy. I'll be walking away from something that was a lifelong dream, something I worked hard to attain. But it won't be the end of the world. I have a great love for the game. I look around and see so many truly great players who may be in the Hall of Fame, but they never got to experience the thrill of being in a playoff situation or of winning a Super Bowl. I really feel I've been more than amply rewarded. I've been blessed. But I have to realize that with all this—with all the trophies and the awards and the recognition and whatever accomplishments there are—this is only the breakfast of my life. Once in a while I may think I'm getting the main course. But the real treat, the dessert, comes at the end of the line, when I get my reward from God.

I have experienced a great joy in living, and I love life, but all these are temporary things. They'll pass someday. They're all very tangible and physical and, compared with the joy of being a child of God, they really don't amount to much. All I want is to live life to the fullest, the way the Lord wants me to live it, to give to others, to share that joy with others, and to be an example and spread the Word in the way He chooses for me. I think God wants me to witness for Him in a cynical world where maybe a lot of people want a football player to talk about x's and o's and trap plays. These people think that being a Christian eliminates the fun from living. I can testify that my life only started being fun when I formed a new relationship with the Lord and made Him first in my life.

The most assuring thing to me is the knowledge that when I'm through with football, I'll still have my faith in God. I know that when it's time for a decision to be made about what I am to do with the rest of my years, He'll give me the guidance and direction I need. The same way He helped me through crises before.

At this stage of my career, I'm not consumed with worry about the boos I'll get. Hey, I'm going to get booed! I know that. I accept that. I may not like it, but I've realized that's part of the game. I can live with it. When I got criticized before— and there were times when people came right up to me in the parking lot, on the street, or in a restaurant, and one time I got it from someone right in the garage where I park my car—I took it home with me and brooded over it. But as I gained maturity and had a little success, I developed a hardness to all that. I don't think it's a cold hardness, but rather a mental toughness that enables me to live with criticism and occasional failure. These things don't affect my performance any longer. They used to.

I'm working now to develop my voice, because I want to pursue a career as a country singer. I grew up with the music, and it's part of me. It would be easy now for me to jump out and capitalize on my football career, and I think people would come out to hear me sing. I did it a little bit before, but I wasn't ready. I wasn't properly prepared; I didn't have the schooling. I didn't do a very good job and I know it. I was just out having fun and meeting lots of people. But I want to be good at singing when I try it again. It's a lot like football in that it takes a lot of time to develop. I've hired a producer who's working with me, and I've made a commitment so that if down the road it doesn't work, at least I'll be able to say I gave it my very best effort.

And I want to raise horses and cattle and do both successfully. I love animals and the land. I did a bit in a movie with Burt Reynolds, but I know I'm not going to rush out and pursue an acting career. I'm just gonna be myself, and if something happens in the way of an acting career, then we'll check it out. I guess what I'm saying is that whatever I do, I want to do it well and not just jump in somewhere because I happen to be a football player.

I have tried not to set specific goals. Just one goal is of great importance to me, and that one is eternal life. Maturing as a Christian helps me to understand that we really shouldn't worry about the treasures we might lay up for ourselves on earth. There's a much better life waiting, and that's the one that counts.

Witnessing

16 Of all the things I do in life, the single most important function is to witness for Jesus Christ. As a small boy I had Bible study at home and I went regularly to Sunday school, but the Bible never took on significant meaning to me until 1974. It wasn't until then that I began a real search for the message of the Lord. My real growth as a Christian can be measured from that time. Like many other people, as I've studied the Word, I have found a favorite passage of Scripture:

"Whosoever therefore shall confess me before men, him will I confess also before my Father, which is in heaven" (Matthew 10:32).

That same message can be found in Luke 12:8. If you check the verses following that one in each case, it's pretty clear that if a person denies Jesus before men, Jesus will then deny that person in front of God. Some areas of the Bible are kind of confusing to me, but there's certainly no gray area here. In the tenth chapter of Romans, Paul is very specific about our Christian duties; in the second chapter of Philippians we're told to do all things for the glory of God and not to bring any credit to ourselves.

All through the Bible the orders are clear. If we call ourselves Christians, if we believe Jesus died for our sins and that

He is coming again, then we must obey Him. And we're supposed to pray, praise, and preach. Now, this isn't to say that all
people can get up in front of a crowd and do an effective job of
telling others about the Lord. For a long time I felt I had a
calling to the ministry; I had terrible guilt about not going to
divinity school. But through some pretty sound counseling
and my own soul-searching, I became convinced that I can be
perhaps an even more effective witness through professional
football.

Many times young people will come to me and say,
"Terry, I see you doing it, but I just can't get up there and
witness in front of other people." I'm far from a Bible scholar,
but I tell them that as far as I can determine, God wants all His
children to witness. And there are many ways to accomplish
this. Certainly the most effective way is through the kind of
life you lead and the kind of conduct you show the world.
Someone once said that the best sermons are lived and not
preached, anyway.

Even as a young Christian I was never bashful about
standing up in front of others and witnessing. Maybe the
toughest thing to learn to accept as a baby Christian is that if
you are a born-again Christian, you will find lots of people
who liked the old you better than the new you. They'll taunt
and jeer and make fun of you because they cannot accept the
new person living inside you. When I was going through my
most difficult times in my personal life—and there are some
tough times I'm going through right now—I knew long before
any of my critics did that I wasn't living the Bible nearly as
successfully as I was talking about it. People had every right to
scorn me and make fun of me.

Guilt is something that all of us have with us. Guilt lays a
little heavier on us when we really do know right from wrong,
when we've professed our faith in Christ and we've fallen
down. I don't ever want anyone to think that I'd equate myself
in any way with the troubles the Lord had, but it tells us in the
Bible that He did some of His greatest works in places where
people refused to repent, even after seeing these miracles. He
was called crazy, a drunkard, a glutton; He was maligned,
denied, and betrayed; and finally He died for our sins.

We are made in His image and we seek to be like Him. But even the disciples He chose to be with Him from the very beginning let Him down terribly. They went to sleep when He was in the Garden. They denied knowing Him. And when He was on the cross, only one of the disciples remained there with Him. It's truly amazing to me that the hand-picked Twelve, who saw firsthand the things He did and the miracles He worked, could have behaved in such a way. Maybe we should ask ourselves, as believers, how we would have behaved under those circumstances. Would we have denied knowing Him if we thought our lives were threatened? Would we have fallen asleep when He asked us to rise and pray so that we wouldn't fall into temptation? If someone came up to me today and said "Terry, do you love the Lord enough to die for Him right now?" would I have the courage to give up my life? I think we have to test our faith that way. Yet we are taught if we lose our life for His sake, that's when we really find our life.

The human heart is a hard thing, and we're all selfish by nature. The Bible is filled with stories about people who did everything in the world to keep from giving themselves over to God. The beauty of studying the Bible is understanding that He knows we are human, that we make mistakes, that we are sinful by nature, that we stumble and fall. Yet He loves us. We are disciples, and a good preacher friend of mine told me that this means that we are under the discipline of Christ. Early in my faith, I just didn't understand why a Christian couldn't be perfect. Those were very emotional times for me, when I was in college and going around doing my missionary work. I was so zealous and wanted to be just the best Christian the world has ever known. I guess you could say I wanted to be a Superstar Christian. And when I fell short, I was all torn up inside. Then I'd think about dying, and I thought God was just waiting to punish Terry Bradshaw for doing something wrong.

I'll never confess to being a dumb quarterback, but back then I was really a dumb Christian. All I thought about was the wrath of God and not nearly enough about the goodness and mercy of God. I've found out that being a Christian is not the easiest thing in the world. This is an awful society in many ways, with many cults and false prophets and young people going off in many different directions. I've learned that Jesus Himself tells us that rather than being easy, it would be tough to follow Him.

If I could make a comparison between becoming an effective Christian and becoming an effective quarterback, perhaps this would express how I feel. It took me nine years to become an accepted quarterback in the National Football League. It was very difficult; I had to endure a lot of pain and not just the physical kind. I had to dedicate myself to certain goals; I had to study and work hard. I think I'm on the road to being an effective Christian, a good witness who perhaps could be instrumental in leading someone down the right path. I wasn't what you'd call a gifted athlete. Throwing the football has not been easy for me. I was slow in maturing, slow with my motor coordination. But the Lord blessed me with such a desire to succeed and such a willingness to work that I was able to dedicate myself to attain a certain goal. I knew I wasn't good, but I wanted to be good. So I worked at it, and I still work at it. And now I'm accepted in football. Believe me, I have that same dedication to being a Christian of the kind that will cause the Lord to look at me and accept me and think I've done a pretty fair job.

I have the approval I've always wanted in football; I want it in my fellowship with God too. I know I can't get it through good works and all that, and I understand that it comes only through the mercy of God. But I know He expects things from me, as one of His children. We can sing at the top of our lungs that old hymn "Stand Up, Stand Up for Jesus," but unless we're willing to stand up when it counts—in public, in front of everyone no matter what the circumstances are—then we aren't being effective witnesses for Him. We can't be bashful about saying "I love the Lord." We have to say it, and mean it, and then prove it.

*O*n a bright spring morning in March of 1979, Terry Bradshaw was up at dawn. While some of his guests slept, he was drinking coffee and studying. He had studied some during the week, and then on Saturday, while working in the fields at his ranch, he had decided what to tell the teenagers he would address during Sunday school at the First Baptist Church in Mansfield, Louisiana. Mansfield is a small town just a piece down the road from Terry's Circle 12 Ranch near Holly.

Early this Sunday, Terry was reading the Bible, searching for key passages. He was going through an assortment of books and pamphlets he has collected along the way which help him find Scripture aids for such occasions. He had decided to dress casually: "I'm not too comfortable in a tie, and besides, all these young people know who I am. I'm just one of them, that's all." And this is how Terry Bradshaw—the National Football League's player of the year, most valuable player in Super Bowl XIII, and boy-next-door—witnessed on an early spring morning in Louisiana:

I've been asked to come here this morning and share with you some thoughts I have about witnessing. I've been witnessing for a lot of years. I've been a Christian for a long time; I accepted Christ as my Savior when I was nine years old. For a long time, I didn't really understand what witnessing meant. To me, witnessing meant going out and communicating with people and telling them about something about which they may or may not have heard. But when I was a senior in high school and became the starting quarterback for Woodlawn High in Shreveport, a youth minister came and told me that I had a great opportunity, as an athlete, to use the football field as an area of witness for Jesus Christ. The truth of that never really registered with me until I went to Louisiana Tech. There I really got involved in witnessing, and I did it all through college. And it occurred to me then that maybe a few people will listen to me because I am a football player. I thought maybe I could be an instrument of the Lord, and maybe He'd use me in this special way because, after all, it was the Lord who blessed me with whatever talents I have.

Then I found a beautiful passage of Scripture—Matthew 10:32—and it says, "Whosoever therefore shall confess me before men, him will I confess also before my Father which is in heaven." What this means to me is that Jesus is saying to every one of His children that He'll trade with you—He's saying, "Here, if you tell others what it's like to be a Christian, how wonderful it is, what joy it gives you, what peace of mind it gives you, how it enriches your life and how much you love Me, and how good it feels to know that you're saved and that your sins are paid for—if you'll just do that much for Me, I'll do ten times that much in your behalf in front of God."

In Matthew 5:16 Jesus said, "Let your light so shine before men, that they may see your good works, and glorify your Father which is in heaven." To me, that means Jesus wants us to speak out, to stand up, and to make certain that other people can look at us and the way we live and recognize the fact that we're saved, that we're Christians. I'm not talking about just *being* a Christian. I can't say, "Well, I'm saved, so I don't want to do any work for Jesus. I don't want to be burdened with the job of sharing the good news about Christ. All I want to do is play football, raise my horses, tend to my cattle, and drive around in my old truck." Being saved doesn't mean that we have no responsibilities. When you accept Christ, you take on some pretty heavy obligations.

God blessed me with the ability to be a football player. Because of that, I get an audience—someone listens when a star athlete speaks. I'm not saying I'm a star—I'm just saying that I've been lucky, and a lot of people know who Terry Bradshaw is because of football. And a lot of young men idolize football players: they want to be like them. But I have a responsibility to those young people and, more than that, I have a responsibility to God. Being a professional athlete is great. I love it! It's been good to me. But I owe it to God to get up here this morning and tell you that all these good things I enjoy today are the result of the blessings Terry Bradshaw has received from God.

Now, some of you may feel that you cannot do what I'm doing today. You may say to yourself, "I can't get up there and speak in front of people"—and maybe you can't. God prepares the hearts of all of us. He gives us different talents. But all of us have obligations if we claim Him as our Savior. God has a purpose for everyone and He knows what we can do, better than we ourselves know. And I don't think He'd have done for me all the things He has done unless He knew that I could handle them. The very least thing that I can do for Him while

I'm on this earth is to tell you what Jesus means to me and to share with you my experiences and whatever knowledge I have about being a Christian.

A few years ago, when I was picked for the All-America team in college, I had big write-ups and got my name and picture in all the magazines and was the first player drafted by the National Football League—and, well, I thought I was really getting to be somebody. I was all wrapped up in myself. I said to myself, "Boy I really got it made." I was becoming famous, and I immediately started putting Him to the side and putting myself on top. I was very selfish, full of myself. Everything I was doing was for Terry Bradshaw, not for the glory of the King of Heaven. I was saved; I was a Christian. But my ego got in the way, and I had myself on the throne. I was growing as a football player and not at all as a Christian. I isolated myself from God.

One day I couldn't stand it any longer. I had quit praying and reading the Bible—and one day I started both those things again. The first thing I did was to ask forgiveness for my selfishness. It was a struggle. It was struggle, struggle, struggle; pray, pray, pray; and struggle some more. I had to come from behind, you might say. I had to convince God I was serious. Then one day, bingo! I felt that presence again. I felt as if I was back on the track.

Once I started my rookie season in the National Football League and thought I had things all together again, I got sidetracked again. In the next couple of years I was running all around the country doing television shows and commercials, dating beautiful women, meeting a lot of big-time people—and it happened again. I did the very same thing again. I was having a ball—for four years in the NFL I had a ball. Sure, I was doing some *talking* about Christianity—but not much *living*. I had myself back on that old throne again. I'd knocked God off there once more. Then God knocked me down a few notches and gave me some problems that I just couldn't handle by myself. I was in real danger of being "super flop" instead of Super Bowl. But God knew what was inside me. He knew my potential, and I don't mean just my potential as a quarterback: He knew my potential as a Christian. God knows all our hearts. He knows what's inside. He knows what you and I are really like, not just what we pretend to be. And if you'll open your heart and your life to Him, and give Him a chance to work in your life, He'll make you the happiest person on the face of the earth. He'll provide all the answers for all the questions you have. He'll do it at His own pace.

It took me nine years to get accepted as a good quarterback in the NFL. Nine years! Nine long years! God knew it'd take nine years. He was the One who was patient: I was impatient. He knew that all the suffering I went through as a young professional was for a reason. He knew, when I couldn't understand it, that all the booing, all the ups and downs, the benching, the being pulled from games, the being shouted at on national TV were important and necessary for me to grow as a Christian. And when He felt I was ready for being known and accepted as a good quarterback, He gave that to me. He did it in His good time, not mine.

But you know, nine years isn't a very long time when we think of spending eternity with God. Our whole lives here on earth amount to such a little bit when compared to forever with Him. Don't waste your time. Don't blow it. Don't blow the chance to be a Christian, to be fulfilled, to let Christ enrich your life. Being a Christian doesn't mean not having fun; being a Christian means having more enjoyment out of life than you ever dreamed possible. It's not a toy you can play with. Being a Christian is very serious business. Jesus said it wasn't gonna be easy, and it isn't. Your friends may laugh at you; they may make fun of you. But remember, Jesus said He was coming not as a peacemaker, but bearing a sword. He said we'll be killed for His sake. Sometimes when you try to share the joy of Christ with someone else, that person will tell you you're nuts. That's all right—lots of people thought Jesus was crazy too. But He is the answer for everything. And when you get in trouble or in a spot and you need strength, He'll be right there to give it to you.

One of the hardest things in the world to do is to go to a friend of yours—maybe a really neat person, a great friend, but one who's unsaved—and try to witness to that person. But you have a responsibility to do that. It's hard sometimes for me to be the good Christian example that I should be. But believe me, God understands our weaknesses. He understands mine. He knows we're gonna fail and stumble around and make giant mistakes. But He loves us all the way, no matter what. He knows what it's like to be tempted. He suffered all the things that we do, and a lot more. There's lots of sin on this old earth. The devil is moving around along with the Holy Spirit, and it's a constant battle raging. You have to make decisions all the time. You'll come to crossroads, and you and you alone will have to decide which way to turn. But if you have Christ in your life, He'll be there to help you even when you make the wrong decisions and the wrong turns.

If I could lay one thing on you, it would be that I went through a time when I was ashamed to call myself a Christian. I turned away from God, but you young people have to know that not one time did God ever turn away from me. Not one time did He let me down. I let Him down plenty.

God didn't change. God never changes. People change. I can go around and say that God didn't reveal Himself to me, but that's being ridiculous: God was there all the time! I was just so concerned with myself that I never gave my faith a chance to work for me. To do that, you have to pray and search the Word. The Word gives you answers and gives you strength and gives you patience for the trials of the world. God is not of this world. And the great thing is that we can live with Him forever if we but dedicate ourselves to it and abide by His will and not always be concerned with what *we* want, but rather what *He* wants for us. Part of what He wants from Terry Bradshaw is witnessing.

Don't throw away the great opportunity to help others to know Christ personally. The best way they can know how you feel is by the way you live. Don't be ashamed to say that you love Christ; don't be afraid to witness; don't be afraid to express your feelings; and don't worry if you think you aren't always saying the right words. God will lead you and direct you in the path that He has chosen for you. God will use each of His people in a very special way, in His own time. The more you give yourself to Him and let Him control your life, the more He'll use you and the happier life you'll have.

My Way, Her Way, His Way

17 By now the whole world must know that Jo Jo and I haven't made an overwhelming success out of our marriage. We've talked openly about it on national television, and we've opened ourselves up in national magazine articles.

Sometimes I think if I had it all to do over again, I'd just keep my mouth shut. But that would be totally against the grain for me. I cannot lie, and when someone asks me a direct question, it's never been my style to be cute. I try never to dodge a question and always to give an honest answer, and I've fielded some tough and, at times, embarrassing questions.

I have to be honest here, too. I've been reluctant to talk about this part of my life for this book and did a lot of soul-searching and praying before getting into it. But the bottom line is always the same for me: Go straight ahead, letting everything loose and putting everything on the line and taking my chances on what happens after that. I'm not a fancy quarterback and not very fancy when it comes to more personal matters. Sometimes I don't like what I see in print after I say something, but I never yell and protest about being misquoted.

No one feels lukewarm about me on the football field, and since Jo Jo and I have aired our problems in public, I have come to the conclusion that no one feels lukewarm about me in this matter either. The women's libbers will all line up against me, and the good, down-home, old-fashioned women will be in my corner. As for the men, most of them will be for me, except for the handful who've given up the traditional male role.

And before we proceed, I'll answer the most obvious question that will pop up after you've read much further. You'll want to know why the two of us didn't take time to sit down and discuss all these things before we got married, in order that we might have headed some of the problems off at the pass. The answer is that for the most part we did discuss many of the issues that have come between us, and we thought we had most of them resolved. As for the others, we were so very much in love—still are, for that matter—it never occurred to us they'd ever become a problem of any consequence.

Our basic problem is that I want my wife with me—I want her at my side, raising our children, putting our family ahead of everything except for our fellowship with God. I'm a down-home boy from Louisiana and that's where I want to spend all my time when I'm not playing football for the Pittsburgh Steelers. Okay, I'm a male chauvinist! I said it, so you don't have to. More than that, I'm not ashamed of being that! I think that for the most part, a woman's place is in the home. Jo Jo had a career when I married her, and I never want to rob her of her identity and take away anything she's worked and sacrificed to accomplish. But there comes a time—not only with figure skating but with football—when you should re-arrange your priorities and get your house in order, so to speak, and start thinking about what you really want to do for the rest of your life. She can't skate forever, and I can't play football forever. But we can live together forever, and I want to do that. And we can raise a family together, and I want to do that when both of us know that our train is on the tracks and that it'll suffer no derailment.

I'm thirty-one and Jo Jo is twenty-eight, and we're at the time in our lives when we should be able to take a mature approach to whatever problems we have. We've spent thousands of hours praying together, reading the Bible together, and talking and getting into spats in an effort to work things out. This much is for sure: We love the Lord and we love each other. But we've had some high mountains to climb. And we've talked with several so-called experts on marriage. One fine Christian counselor we both know told us he didn't even want to discuss the problems with us because to his way of thinking, we both were selfish. That took care of that.

Because of my frankness, I guess everyone in the Steeler organization knew last year that we were struggling. When Jo Jo left last fall to begin rehearsing for *Ice Dancing* on Broadway, I was beside myself. I couldn't bear the thought of being without the woman I love, and it tore me apart. And when something is bothering me, I don't have very good methods for hiding it. So I went straight to Coach Noll and told him that my personal life wasn't all that I'd like it to be. We had a tremendous talk, and he let me know that he understood. And the Rooney family couldn't have been nicer. Almost every week Mr. Rooney (Art Sr., who owns the Steelers) would invite me to his home for dinner. Usually it was on Thursday night. We didn't even talk football. He made me feel like part of the family. I must have felt pretty much at home, too, because sometimes after eating I'd flop down on the couch and go to sleep. I hung around the stadium more than ever before, simply because there wasn't any reason to go home.

Once in a while when Jo Jo would come home for a day, she'd go out and buy groceries and load up the refrigerator. Then until she'd come back home the next time, I'd get by mainly on soup and sandwiches and some bacon and eggs. I'll admit, I'm not much of a cook. And I hate to go out and sit alone in a restaurant.

Now, at the time we were getting ready to take on the Cowboys in the Super Bowl, anybody who didn't know about our problems and the tensions in our household found out about them then. A writer for a national magazine interviewed me, and I said exactly what was on my mind: That the management of Jo Jo's Broadway show wasn't interested in her feelings, or mine, or anybody's problems; that I was lonely and depressed; that the long separations were hard on our marriage; and that we'd have to think long and hard on it and make certain we had a solid marriage before starting to raise a family. The headline on the article said something about me being so lonesome I could cry when Jo Jo skates off. Well, that's an old line out of a Hank Williams song, and that's exactly how I feel when we're apart.

I've confessed to being a sad-song freak. Always have been. I love some lines out of one of Larry Gatlin's songs—he's truly a great friend of mine: ". . . So lay back down and love me, and leave the leaving to later on. . . . I don't want to cry." And I used to listen all the time to the lines "The heart is a funny thing, with a mind all its own; it withers like a garden, left untended, and alone." I can really identify with that.

It's one thing to read Scripture over the phone with each other and to share Bible passages and prayer. But I'd rather do those things in person with my wife at my side. The magazine article was absolutely correct. And I'm sure there were lots of women who were turned off by it. I was very lonely and I admitted it. If that's a male chauvinist talking, so be it. All the article said was, Hey, my wife is gone and isn't here when I need her and I want her here and she's off skating and I understand those needs for her to fulfill her talents. I understand them. I agree with them. I'm not trying to stop her from doing her thing and wouldn't ever do it. But I don't have to like it. It's the difference between accepting something and understanding it, and wanting and liking that same thing.

I told Jo Jo before the article was published that she wouldn't like it. But it made her out to be the heroine, and I was the villain. And that's all right. I can't hide my true feelings. Maybe it would sound all peaches and cream if I said, That's great, I'm glad she's gone. If I said I thought it was terrific that she's bouncing around Europe doing something and then New York and then Los Angeles, I'd be lying. A marriage has to be formed in the home, not on the telephone. If I were the kind of guy who wanted to be flitting all around the world all the time, and married to a woman who wanted to be running off in another direction doing her thing—well, how sad! Then we could just stay apart and soon we'd have no reason in the world to ever be together.

Family life is very important to me. I grew up in a family

wound pretty tight by love and mutual respect, and I need that. I learned a long time ago that a strong family life and a strong church-centered life are things that keep people together. Now, if some modern, liberated outfit wants to say this makes Terry Bradshaw a bad guy, that's too bad! You can't live in two different worlds (there's an old song about that) and you know what happens when two worlds collide (hey, there's another reminder from a song). You have to live together and pray together and read the Bible together and go to church together and raise kids together.

I was by myself for all practical purposes for six months in the last calendar year. I saw my wife once every few weeks, and that simply isn't enough for me. I was broken-hearted all year long. I cried my heart out. I was so alone and so miserable and so jealous. Yes, I was jealous of the fact that she was more wrapped up in her skating and in Broadway and that life style than she was in her husband.

You see, I married a West Coast woman. She loves California. She loves New York City. She loves ballet, I like square dancing. She loves the opera, I like the Grand Ole Opry. She loves bright lights, and I like the soft moonlight of the ranch. She's just having a hard time adjusting to the simple way of life. I'm a simple person. Maybe I'm dull and unimaginative, but everything I like in life is pretty uncomplicated. If I had my way, I'd sit right here on this ranch and hardly ever leave, except to go and play football. And Jo Jo is so very much accustomed to another way of life. The ranch is very low-key and slow-paced for her. There's nothing for her to do, and she doesn't have any friends down here. She thinks differently than the people down here think. It's not her fault, and it's not their fault. But I tell her that if she'd just give it a chance down here, and try to accustom herself to this way of life and the people, well, she'd blend right in. She thinks of it as being stuck out here in the sticks. I mean, there's a whole lot of difference between Broadway and Holly, Louisiana.

If you're used to Hollywood and the bright lights of Broadway, I'm sure it's pretty scary to think of spending your life down here.

*I*t's a thirty-minute ride from Shreveport to Terry Bradshaw's Circle 12 Ranch—which really is near Holly, yet the mail comes to a post office in Grand Cane. The last five or six minutes make for a bumpy ride over the red clay road made more uncomfortable by the spring rains. This is flatland country, dotted by tiny settlements like Frierson and Kingston. There are perhaps sixty or seventy people living in those places. Once in a while you'll see a once-stately old house that used to be a plantation. There are sharecroppers' cottages everywhere.

I bought this place six or seven years ago. My dad found it for me. I wanted to get out into the country. I've always had a great love for the land. I love animals. As a kid I dreamed of having a place in the country where I could raise animals. I simply wanted to have a place where I could get away from everything. I bought this place the first day I saw it—I just fell in love with it. I couldn't afford it at the time, but I bought it anyway.

For two years things weren't handled right, then my Uncle Bobby and Aunt Margie decided they'd like to live here, and ever since then it's been great. Once Jo Jo and I got married, she went through and fixed things the way we wanted them. It's come a long way. At the beginning, the payments on this place were about as much as I was making, but we got it all worked out. The Lord blessed us and took care of us. This is like having a little bit of heaven right here on earth.

When we come here, I start absorbing everything around me. I really thirst for the place. I get goose-bumps all over. And when we come here, I can see a change in Jo Jo too, but it's as if the world is closing in on her. She's okay for a few days, then she gets the urge to get out and go somewhere. It's like she can't really be happy here. And I couldn't ever be happy anywhere else.

*T*here is a little knoll not far from the main house, and each morning Terry Bradshaw grabs a cup of coffee and jumps in his battered Jeep and sits on that knoll for his Bible study and prayer.

*E*veryone needs a place where he can go to forget the cares of the world, and this is my place. The folks down here know me and they're mighty nice people. But if I don't want anyone from the outside world to bother me, then I can really disappear down here. And I honestly feel closer to God. I know God is everywhere, but it seems I can almost reach out and touch Him here. There's so much that is beautiful about nature, and I have a much better view of the wonderful things He created. Distractions can sometimes get between God and His people, but this is an uncluttered atmosphere for me. I'm much more aware of His presence. Maybe it doesn't mean much to people who were raised in a city and who like that kind of pace, but one of the most thrilling things in the world is the birth of a little calf or a baby horse. I just suck this place in like a sponge—I can't get enough of it. There are things I want to do and improvements I want to make. It's no mansion, but it's my home, the first one I've ever owned, and it's very much a part of me. It's a place where I want to put down roots, and I've done it except for raising kids here.

Jo Jo isn't ready to put her roots down here. I have a natural tendency to rebel against that, and to say, "Hey, this is our home. I'm providing for you. I'm taking care of you." I'm from the old school. I believe that a woman should be with a man wherever he is, whether it's Louisiana or Timbuktu. You see, when we talked about these things before we got married, Jo Jo said she was tired of skating, tired of traveling. She wanted to settle down and have a family. She knew this is where I wanted to be. But I knew as soon as she got here she couldn't stay for long. And then she found out she really didn't want to retire as such. Maybe she didn't want to perform night after night, but she has a need to perform. Sometimes I think that's when she is happiest.

I have to remember that she's been doing that for almost all her life. Her mother raised her alone from the time Jo Jo was four years old and she got an early taste of show business. She's been in those lights and she's heard that applause, and she found out she missed it when she didn't have it. Being a wife and a mother wasn't going to be enough. And having a part-time wife just isn't enough for me. She wants us to live either in California or in New York, and I just can't hack that. We've studied the Bible through and through, looking for answers, and I'll find passages about the responsibilities of each party. And it says in the Bible that a woman is supposed to be submissive to the man. He makes the living. He takes care of her. Jo Jo has all the freedom in the world to do outside things. Not many women have that. All I ask of her is that she not put pressure on me as to where we'll live. God knows we've tried to work it out, but we have these pressures coming at us from different directions. It's just as hard for her to change as it is for me. We're two people, apart too much, who love the Lord, and we've made a mess out of some things. And only our great love for the Lord and for each other has kept us together.

This past season was just terrible. How things went so well on the field is amazing in itself. I buried myself in my work. I went to practice early and stayed late. I hated coming home: the apartment was empty; I was empty. My prayer life was very strong, yet I was extremely confused. I understood what was going on, yet the natural man inside of me was yelling out that I was being short-changed in my marriage. Where's my wife? Why isn't she with me where she belongs? I was jealous of the fact that she was loving what she was doing. I felt she had made a choice, that she would rather be a star on Broadway than be the wife of Terry Bradshaw. I felt she was being Jo Jo Starbuck, not Jo Jo Bradshaw. And I was jealous of the guy she was skating with. Now, I don't think for one minute that either one of us has ever had a single thought about being unfaithful. Jo Jo simply touched on emotions that I had never experienced before.

When I went to see Jo Jo in the show—well, it just killed me. It killed me because she was enjoying it so much. I didn't want to hear how much fun she was having. What I wanted to hear was "Honey, I miss you so much. I can't stand being separated from you. Let's go to the ranch." That's what I wanted to hear, but I didn't hear it. I know in my heart she loved me and that she was doing her thing, just as I do mine in football. But all I could think about was Hollywood, Hollywood. The couples out there don't make it because there are two stars traveling in different directions. And when Jo Jo and I would have our little bit of time together, she'd be talking about Broadway and maybe having a career as an actress, and I'd be talking about football. Then we'd wind up talking about our problems, and then the talking became arguing. I've been ashamed of myself for some of the jealousy and resentment I've felt, but pardner, I'm open and up front about it. I love this woman. She's gorgeous, she's sweet, she's kind, and most of all she's a good Christian woman. I just want a full-time wife, that's all. And in the final analysis, I don't think that's too much to ask.

Jo Jo thinks it is, at least right now. She is a lovely human being who is torn between her responsibilities as a wife and the desire to fulfill herself as a skater and/or actress as much as she can. She cringes, too, when she sees some of the remarks she and Terry make so forthrightly appear in print. And she worries a great deal about what the two careers might do to her marriage:

"Terry and I love each other so much, but there's more to life than being Suzy Homemaker. That's fine, to a point. But that's not all there is to it. I was very naïve when we got married. I did all those little things like giving him breakfast in bed and fussing over him, but I never got the feeling he really appreciated it. Maybe I expected more approval. But he didn't jump up and down with joy and, frankly, I was bored. When I had a chance to perform, I grabbed it.

"Maybe because of the different life styles we had when we were children, the separations haven't had the effect on me they have had on Terry. I hate being away from my friends and I have a variety of interests. Terry doesn't understand that. I really believe that absence can make the heart grow fonder. I miss Terry when we're apart, but I have my friends to fall back on. I love going out to dinner and talking with them. Terry doesn't do that. He goes home and he's alone. And then he pouts and sulks and gets angry and jealous. You see, I know what he's going through. When I was with Ice Capades, I did the same thing: I performed, then I went back to an empty hotel room.

"I couldn't stand just having a career with no home life and no love life. I need all those things. Terry wants me home—period. But sometimes when I'm there, he seems to take me for granted. And after a few days at the ranch, I go out of my mind. It's so far from everything, and there's nothing for me to do except putter around the house. I'm all right as long as I know I have something to look forward to, a trip that'll get me out of there. But I didn't grow up in a cooped-up atmosphere, and I can't make that adjustment. I want to be a good wife to Terry, but he has that Southern background, and if you ask him, he'll admit he's a chauvinist. And I've always had to be pretty independent, because my mother raised me by herself since my dad died when I was just four years old. Terry doesn't want a woman to be independent. He wants someone to be totally dependent on him—that's the kind of women he grew up with. His mom was happy just to stay home and take care of her men, but for me, that's a pretty thankless job. I need more than that. I'm confident of Terry's love for me, but I don't have to stay home every day just to prove it. And I don't take him for granted.

"He gets jealous when I go out to dinner with my friends. But he knows I'm faithful to him, just as I know he's faithful to me. When I opened on Broadway, I got flowers and messages from a lot of people, but not a word from the person who meant most to me. Maybe it was Terry's way of protesting, of telling me he didn't like what I was doing. Then sometimes when we talk on the phone, the warmth is missing and I know he's resentful. He gets very defensive. We've talked until we're both blue in the face and I've tried to make Terry understand that we don't have to smother each other nor stifle each other's outside interests.

"For a marriage to work, especially when there are two careers involved, you need an extraordinary amount of compassion and understanding and love. You really do have to want the best for the other person. I certainly want the best for Terry in his career. I just wish he felt the same way about mine. I wish he'd be more supportive as I try to develop my career. Sometimes last fall I would have just one day off, and I would have felt a whole lot better if I could have stayed in bed all day and rested. But I knew Terry needed me, so I jumped on a plane and went to be with him. Yet sometimes he didn't seem to appreciate it. He'd be indifferent, pouting—I guess because he had been alone.

"We're both trying very hard to do the right thing and to work things out. It's very difficult, I know, for both of us. We're both trying to understand the other's situation. I guess neither of us had much of an idea what it would be like. Terry has said that if he knew it'd be like this, he'd never have gotten into it. He says someone in the family has to dominate and that it's going to be him. Well, I don't want to be dominated. What I want more than anything else is his support and under- standing and appreciation. Neither one of us is getting the things out of the marriage that we thought we would. All we can do is keep working at it. We have to keep talking with each other about our problems. We have to keep praying and hop- ing. We just have to put our lives in His hands and trust God to give us the answers we haven't found for ourselves."

There have been times when I have deliberately ig- nored Jo Jo. And that just made matters worse. She'd come in and start crying because I wasn't understanding, and then I'd tell her if she had been home where she belonged there'd be no reason for either of us being upset. That's the child in me—I know that. She'd tell me how other folks told her how pretty she is, how nice she looks in such and such a costume, and what a good skater she is and how much applause she gets. I'd hear all that and I'd think, "Do you really need all that?" and the answer would be, "I guess she does need it."

When we were apart, we'd wear out the telephone. We kept the lines of communication open, and we read some beautiful and meaningful Scripture passages to each other. And my, how we prayed over the phone! But still, I was in one place and she was in another. At night, I'd be tossing and turning and trying to sleep, just waiting for her to call after her show was over. If she didn't call right away, I'd be upset. Sometimes she'd cut the conversation short, telling me she was going to run out and have dinner with her friends. And that would make me angry all over again. Jo Jo was brought up in a world where she was made to believe that everything's sugar and spice. It's not a real world—it's like Disneyland. She was used to being pampered, put on a pedestal. And I guess I knocked the pedestal out from under her. My world is the real world. Sure, I'm used to Southern women and the way they treat their men. That's my heritage. My world isn't all Santa Claus and the Easter Bunny and costumes and spotlights and applause. I'd like to think I'm a very practical person. I feel very fortunate to have done as well as I have, and I'm anxious to make life as comfortable as possible for everyone I love.

I thought this was what she wanted. She said she was tired of performing: she wanted a home; she wanted a family. Those were exactly the things I wanted. We came down here after our honeymoon, and I'd get up and go to work, cut hay all day, work the cattle and horses, and come back to the house and she'd be twiddling her thumbs, bored to death. When I left to go to training camp, she went to California for six weeks. That was in 1976. Since that time, we really haven't had the time together that I think we need. It's been hit-and-miss. We've spent holidays apart and missed out on much that I feel a husband and wife should have.

We've grown some as a couple, but we have a long way to go. We're grateful to God for the nice things that have happened to both of us, and we know that He's watching over us.

God didn't put either one of us on earth to be miserable. He wants us to be happy in His love. You can't take a situation like this and split it down the middle and say, "Well, Terry wants to live in Louisiana and Jo Jo wants to live in California or New York, so let's split the difference and move to Nebraska." That isn't the answer. The Lord must have the answers. The Bible says every hair on our head is numbered. The Bible says a sparrow does not fall unless God knows about it. So I know He is concerned for us and He wants the very best for us. We've read all the right chapters, the right verses, the love chapter from First Corinthians, and I guess it boils down to the saying that "when there's no way out, there's always a way *up*."

I know we both lack maturity and in many ways are failing

in our Christian witness. But I know, too, that there is a very human side to the Lord. He understands these troubles, and perhaps they are really a cross He's putting on us to make us stronger Christians. Someone told me that just as the strongest steel is forged by the hottest heat, the strongest character is molded by the greatest adversity. If that's the case, Jo Jo and I ought to have one heck of a marriage when we get through all this. The strength and patience we need to get us through will come from the Lord. I've been wanting things my way. Jo Jo wants things her way. Both of us have to stop and listen and wait on the Lord and find out what His way is. I honestly believe He's planted seeds in both of us so that we'll understand His will and then follow the path He lays out for us. All the honors, all the success the world has to offer—these things are pretty empty and shallow if you don't have the peace of the Lord in your heart. Someone handed me a little card one time, and on it were these words: "Blessed is the man who gives up what he can never keep, to gain what he can never lose."

I've collected a few trophies and plaques along the way, and they're scattered all over the place. My folks have some, there are a few in Pittsburgh, and there are some at the ranch. They're nice and I appreciate them, and I know the effort and dedication it took to get them. I've given away two of my Super Bowl rings and don't wear the third. These are earthly things, and to me they're not treasures. I love to compete and I love to win, and maybe there'll be more of that sort of thing down the road.

And I appreciate all that I have. I'm a lucky human being and I know it. As for the struggles, I've had fewer than most. I know what it's like to be a backslider and to be out of fellowship with the Lord. It's strange that since I started a new life in Christ and began to mature as a Christian, I've come to understand that He brings us into deep waters, not to drown us, but to cleanse us. And I know that nothing in this world can separate me from the love of God.

Being certain of that, having the assurance that I'm saved, makes everything worthwhile, makes all trouble bearable, and makes my world brighter than I ever dreamed possible.

Epilogue

hat could top 1978? The Steelers had won it all, winning fourteen of sixteen before reeling off two playoff victories and then edging the Dallas Cowboys for another Super Bowl triumph.

Terry Bradshaw was most valuable player in the Super Bowl. He was named the NFL player of the year by the Associated Press, *Sport* magazine, and the Maxwell Club. Perhaps more important, his own teammates voted him the club's most valuable player. He is the first Steeler to receive the honor twice.

Others may have said it before him, but the late Vince Lombardi said it more frequently: It is much more difficult to stay on top than to get there in the first place.

This was the major problem confronting Coach Chuck Noll when he met with his players for training camp on the campus of St. Vincent College in Latrobe, Pennsylvania, in mid-1979. But the mood was one of optimism short of cockiness. Under Noll, the Steelers had never been a stand-pat team. There were thirty-three rookies on the squad when the drills began in the broiling summer sun. When the team assembled for Super Bowl XIV, a half-dozen were still on the team. And one of those rookies had won two games in overtime with his foot. Besides that, fifteen players on the Steelers' forty-six-man Super Bowl roster had three years' experience or less.

For Terry, coming to training camp was almost a relief. It got him off the merry-go-round existence that comes with being the quarterback of a Super Bowl champion. He had not spent as much time on the ranch as he had hoped. He was fatigued, but it was the wrong kind of fatigue—the kind produced by racing around the country to meet deadlines. The fatigue naturally produced by the rigors of two-a-day practices and seemingly endless meetings would result in dreamless sleep.

Training camp, though, is the same for every player on every team, whether that team won the Super Bowl or finished in last place. A little bit of work goes a long way. Tempers grow short because of the heat and the workouts. The nerve edges get a little tattered with the long separations from family. Every player, on every team, is more than ready for actual combat.

In the preseason exhibition games, the Steelers were 3–1, but the performances were unspectacular. They beat the Buffalo Bills, New York Giants, and New York Jets before losing to the Cowboys in what was billed as "the Super Bowl rematch." The same two teams were playing, all right, but that was the only possible connection with the Super Bowl. The championship feeling simply wasn't there.

The 1979 season began for real the night of September 3 in the Boston suburb of Foxboro. The New England Patriots would be the hosts, and the ABC Monday Night Football television crew would be there. At the outset, the Steelers performed like anything but world champions. The vaunted defense permitted a touchdown the first time the Patriots had the ball. Quarterback Steve Grogan gained generously through the air. New England led 7–0 after the first period.

Jack Lambert's interception set up a Pittsburgh touchdown, but rookie Matt Bahr missed the point-after. The Patriots pounced on a Franco Harris fumble and got the first of two second-period field goals. It was 13–6 at the half.

Neither team could score in the third period. The Steelers then stopped themselves with a fumble at the Patriot 19-yard-line. They got a second chance when a New England punt traveled only 14 yards. Terry completed two passes covering 34 yards—the second one to Sidney Thornton all alone in the middle of the end zone. The fourth quarter ended 13–13.

Bahr atoned for his missed extra-point by hitting on a 41-yard field goal at 5:10 of the overtime period. The Steelers won 16–13. An inartistic opening, but as they say in golf, "it's not how, but how many." Bradshaw hit on 15 of 26 passes for 221 yards and 1 touchdown. He needed to be effective, since the Steelers were playing without six players and lost two more to injuries during the game.

The home opener could not have been more beautiful. The Steelers beat Houston in amazingly easy fashion 38–7. The defense forced 6 turnovers and had a hand in 24 of the 38 points. The key was the job the defense did on Houston running star Earl Campbell, restricting him to a career low of 38 yards in 16 carries.

Terry passed for 2 touchdowns, but had the same number of interceptions, hitting only 12 of 29 for 198 yards. Coach Noll could not have been happy, despite the victory—his team had fumbled 5 times.

And the Steelers were anything but up for the Cardinals in St. Louis a week later. They escaped with a 24–21 triumph, but only after stuffing 17 points into the final quarter. Terry suffered a badly bruised ankle in the first half and wound up with a modest 14 of 31—2 touchdowns but 2 interceptions.

No Steeler team in history had won a dozen games in a row. It was not a healthy team that sought such a record against the Baltimore Colts. The only thing in Pittsburgh's favor was that the game would be played in Three Rivers Stadium. Noll had to start four reserves on defense and three on offense. Franco Harris could not play because of an ankle sprain. Terry was hurt again during the game, but as he has done so many times in the past, he bounced back for a game-saving performance.

Baltimore led 13–10 going into the final period, but the Steelers mounted an 84-yard drive, capped by Bradshaw's 28-yard touchdown pass to Bennie Cunningham. And so, for the third time in four games, the Steelers came from behind in the fourth quarter for a victory. Final score: Steelers 17, Colts 13. Terry was 19 of 30 for 249 yards and 2 touchdowns. He also suffered 2 more interceptions.

The Steelers rallied in the fourth quarter the next Sunday in Philadelphia, too, but the Eagles had built too big a lead. The Steelers turned the football over 4 times, and Terry's 37-yard scoring strike to John Stallworth in the final period wasn't enough. The Eagles won 17–14, breaking the Steelers' 12-game winning streak and tossing the AFC Central Division race into a three-way tie. Terry was 12 for 26, with 176 yards, 1 touchdown, and again 2 interceptions. The first interception was taken back to the Steeler 2-yard-line; the other stopped a drive at the Eagles' 14. And the Steelers still were not a healthy team, playing without five starters on defense.

Franco Harris shook off his injuries and shook loose from his slump the following Sunday in Cleveland before 81,260 fans. The coach had to be happy with the offense that produced 51 points, more than any of his teams had ever put on the scoreboard previously. But he was less than enthusiastic about a defense that yielded 35 points and 458 yards. The Browns' Brian Sipe garnered 365 yards through the air and passed for 5 touchdowns—both records against a Noll-coached team.

The Steelers rushed in front 27–0, scoring on four of their first fifteen plays. Bradshaw threw 3 touchdown passes within the first sixteen minutes. Being so lopsided, it was not a "pretty" victory—a bit mindful of the games in the old American Football League—but it was a victory that put the Steelers back in undisputed possession of first place in their division. Terry was 12 for 21 with 161 yards and 3 touchdowns.

The Steelers played so poorly the following week, they made folks wonder how in the world they ever got to the Super Bowl, even on a pass. They turned the ball over 9 times in a 34–10 loss to a Cincinnati team that had been one of the most inept teams in the NFL through the first six weeks of the season. The Steelers lost the ball on three straight possessions and simply handed the Bengals their first victory of the campaign. There were 9 fumbles (7 of them recovered by Cincinnati) and 2 interceptions, both thrown by Terry. He completed 21 of 40, the most passes he had ever thrown in one game. The bottom line was the most one-sided Steeler loss since 1971.

And the club no longer had the only grip on first place.

The Steelers were quickly becoming one of the game's more unpredictable teams. How could a team that lost by 24 points to a winless Cincinnati team come back the following week and rock Denver by 35? Well, this way: By bolting in front on a Bradshaw-to-Swann pass, by jamming 3 more touchdowns into the second period, by accumulating more than 500 yards in total offense, and by sacking the Bronco quarterback 4 times. Terry had the second-best passing percentage of his career, connecting on 18 of 24 for 267 yards and 2 touchdowns. He was intercepted once.

Now the sportswriters could talk about a Super Bowl match and mean it. The October 28 game in Pittsburgh meant something, with the Dallas Cowboys as the opposition. The Steelers won the old-fashioned way, restricting the Cowboys to 79 yards on the ground and their lowest point production in 108 games.

It was a conservative, structured victory, 14–3. The Steelers gained more yards on the ground than in the air, Harris carrying 18 times and Thornton 14. Terry was 11 for 25 for 126 yards.

Everything came together at Three Rivers on Sunday, November 4. Terry passed for 311 yards, a personal high for one game—and he threw for 4 touchdowns while playing only the first half and one series into the third quarter. It was a 38–7 breeze over the Washington Redskins. And it was an achievement for Coach Noll too. His ninety-sixth victory tied him for fourteenth place on the all-time list alongside Vince Lombardi.

Noll took fourteenth place all to himself the next week in Kansas City. Terry threw for 3 touchdowns in the 30–3 victory over the Chiefs.

Surely the Steelers would never again be as inept as they had been against Cincinnati. Not quite. Against the Chargers in San Diego they were guilty of 8 turnovers instead of 9. It was one of the poorest games of Bradshaw's career. He didn't complete a pass to a wide receiver until the third quarter. He was intercepted 5 times, and 4 of those led directly to San Diego scores. The plane ride back to Pittsburgh seemed longer than some wars.

No one would have thought the Steelers and Browns could put on a wilder performance than the one in Cleveland back in October. Yet the rematch November 25 in Pittsburgh was even more tense. It took Bahr's 37-yard field goal with but nine seconds left in overtime to decide the game in Pittsburgh's favor, 33–30. Terry set a personal single-game high with 30 completions and 364 yards as well as 44 attempts. He completed 9 passes to Franco Harris. But it was a run by Terry, covering 28 yards, that put the Steelers in position to win the game on Bahr's kick. When it was over, the Steelers and Oilers remained in a first-place tie in their division.

December 2 was a day for revenge, and the Steelers got it, beating Cincinnati 37–17. For Terry, it marked the third time in five weeks he had exceeded the 300-yard mark in passing. He riddled the Bengal defense for 339 yards and 2 touchdowns and became the first Steeler to pass for 3,000 yards in a single season.

Pittsburgh could have clinched the division title the following week at Houston, but the Oilers turned an interception into a first-half score and downed the Steelers 20–17. The Steelers clinched a spot in the playoffs, though, and the following week wrapped up the division crown by blanking Buffalo 28–0. So dominant were the Steelers that the Bills had but 1 firstdown rushing. Terry's statistics were 14–27–209 with 1 touchdown and 2 interceptions.

The Steelers had a week to rest before taking on the Miami Dolphins in the AFC playoff game. For Noll, it was a time to return to basics. The Steelers did that flawlessly, controlling the football for 13 minutes of the first period, scoring the first three times they had the ball, and building an insurmountable 20–0 lead. So awesome on defense were the Steelers that Miami gained only 35 yards and had only 4 firstdowns in the first half. Final score: Pittsburgh 34, Miami 14. Bradshaw hit 7 of 9 early on, finished with 21 of 31 for 230 yards and 2 touchdowns (no interceptions), and now it was on to the AFC championship game against the Houston Oilers.

For the Steelers to win, two things were necessary: Terry

Bradshaw had to have a good day, and Earl Campbell had to have a bad one. Final statistics: Bradshaw, 18 of 30 for 219 yards, 2 touchdowns, 1 interception. Campbell, 15 yards in 17 carries. Score: Steelers 27, Oilers 13.

Terry's two scoring passes enabled him to establish an NFL record of 26 touchdown passes in post-season competition. The Steelers had won their sixteenth straight at home and their seventh consecutive playoff game at Three Rivers. Next stop: Pasadena. The date: January 20, 1980. The opposition: The Los Angeles Rams.

Super Bowl games are rarely easy. Teams come out like matadors, jabbing and piercing and poking and trying—more than anything else, not to make the first mistake. They go at each other like classic boxers, settling for the feints and jabs, too conservative to risk the haymaker.

And on this mild, sunny day in the Rose Bowl, the defending Super Bowl champions were playing without two of their defensive stalwarts, Jack Ham and Mike Wagner. It was not the kind of day to favor the Steelers. After all, they had beaten the Dolphins in 24-degree weather, the Oilers when it was 2 degrees colder than that. It was 67 degrees and sunny at kickoff time in Pasadena.

All the pregame hoopla was designed to help the Rams. It seemed as if they needed the help. They were forced to go with an untested quarterback, Vince Ferragamo, who had taken over with five games remaining in the regular season. They were a team geared to defense. They had played in a much weaker division in a decidedly weaker conference. And they were not a "big play" team. In the minds of almost everyone, it was not a question of whether the Steelers would win, but whether the Rams could play well enough to keep the 103,985 fans from dozing off.

At the outset, it appeared it would be exactly that kind of contest—no contest. The Rams twice tried to run the ball. Net loss: 13 yards. Ferragamo passed for 8, bringing up fourth down. The Rams punted.

The Steelers got possession at their own 21-yard-line and then alternated Harris and Rocky Bleier for six plays before Terry hit Harris for a 32-yard pass for a firstdown at the Los

Angeles 26-yard-line. The Steelers settled for Bahr's 41-yard field goal and led 3-0 with but half a period elapsed.

Eight plays later the Rams took the lead on Cullen Bryant's smash up the middle. Wendell Tyler had set up the score with a 39-yard gainer.

This brash display by such an overwhelming underdog did nothing to rattle the Steelers. They simply reasserted themselves and quickly regained the lead. Larry Anderson returned the kickoff 45 yards; Bradshaw hit Cunningham for 8, Swann for 12, Cunningham again for 13, and then Stallworth for 3 and a score just two minutes into the second quarter.

Chuck Noll had tried to warn all the Steelers this was no ordinary game and no ordinary Rams team. Not very many listened. But they all woke up when the Rams added a pair of field goals in the second period. Frank Corral kicked a 31-yarder after a lengthy drive, then David Elmendorf's pickoff of a Bradshaw pass helped the Rams set up Corral's 45-yarder only fourteen seconds before the end of the first half. The Rams, now more determined than ever, led 13–10 at halftime.

The second half was only four plays old when Bradshaw and Swann hooked up on a 47–yard scoring pass. Bahr's conversion shoved the Steelers back on top 17–13.

Less than two minutes later, the Rams were in front once more. Ferragamo hit Billy Waddy on a 50–yarder, setting up a trick play touchdown–Ferragamo handing off to Lawrence McCutcheon, and McCutcheon passing to Smith at the goal line for the go-ahead touchdown. Corral missed the point-after, and the Rams led 19–17.

Twice in the third period the Steelers moved into Los Angeles territory, and twice Terry was intercepted.

The Steelers' first possession of the final period began at their own 25-yard-line. On third and eight, Bradshaw hit John Stallworth at the Rams' 32 and Stallworth, who had gotten behind the defense, completed the 73-yard jaunt. Bahr's conversion made it 24–19 Pittsburgh.

The Rams made one more valiant effort. With 8:29 to play, they moved from their own 16 to the Steeler 32. On first down Ferragamo tried to hit Smith, but Jack Lambert recorded Pittsburgh's one interception of the day. It was the play that killed the Rams. It took the Steelers eight plays to move 70 yards. Franco scored the clincher, and the Steelers won the game 31–19 and again became Super Bowl champions. Terry Bradshaw had his fourth Super Bowl ring, and it was one he could keep for himself.

The Steelers are accustomed to winning. So their locker room is not quite as boisterous as some.

The one following Super Bowl XIV was unique.

There were the customary interviews, the handshakes, and congratulations all around, but Terry Bradshaw was drained—more drained than he ever remembered being. He mentioned quitting. He talked about walking away from the sport. Instead of being elated, he was depressed: the game had taken so much out of him. Instead of feeling supremely confident going into the game, he had grave concerns, perhaps because the Steelers were such an overwhelming favorite.

"I had a lot of negative thoughts going in," he said, "and that's unusual for me. I was really relieved that we won. So I really thought about quitting. I don't recall exactly and precisely what I said, but I know all I could think about was getting away from it all. I felt like running. I didn't want to see a football and didn't want to touch one. Didn't want even to talk about football. I always have a letdown after a big game, but this one was particularly tough. It was a real low."

Wire services hummed with stories about Bradshaw's possible retirement.

Just as quickly, his teammates gathered round him. Joe Greene had a serious chat with Terry. Others talked to him.

Through the night, Terry fought the depression. He looked back on his life, the rough road to the top, the accomplishments, the sacrifices, and the Pittsburgh organization.

"I really thought of calling it quits," he said. "But I realize I love the game, and I think I can contribute for a couple more years at least. I've learned that I shouldn't say anything just after a big game, because the letdown is so great. And it's not a matter of being satisfied with what I've done, because once you get satisfied you are really in trouble."

He peered out from under his ten-gallon hat at the news conference the morning after the Super Bowl triumph. He had the keys to a new automobile, the second in two years since he had again been selected most valuable player in the Super Bowl:

"You know, football is a wonderful way to express my strong belief in God and to spread the faith. Once, at one of these news conferences, I started talking about my faith in God, and I heard a reporter say, 'We're not here to listen to that garbage!' That's too bad, because football is a fleeting thing. The day will come when I'll be called up yonder, and I know there's more to life than football. Really, football is such a small part of the whole thing."

The Bradshaw Record

Position: Quarterback
Team: Pittsburgh Steelers
Birthdate: September 2, 1948
Birthplace: Shreveport, Louisiana

College: Louisiana Tech University
Height: 6-3
Weight: 215
NFL experience: 9 years

How acquired: Draft (first in 1970)

1979   PASSING

Opponent	Att	Comp	Pct	Yds	TD	Int
New England*	26	15	57.7	221	1	0
HOUSTON*	29	12	41.3	198	2	2
St Louis*	31	14	45.2	206	2	2
BALTIMORE*	29	19	65.5	249	2	2
Philadelphia*	26	12	46.1	176	1	2
Cleveland*	21	12	57.1	161	3	0
Cincinnati*	40	21	52.5	275	1	2
DENVER*	24	18	75.0	267	2	1
DALLAS*	25	11	44.0	126	0	0
WASHINGTON*	27	15	55.5	311	4	1
Kansas City*	29	17	58.6	232	3	2
San Diego*	36	18	50.0	153	0	5
CLEVELAND*	44	30	68.1	364	1	1
CINCINNATI*	29	17	58.6	339	2	1
Houston*	29	14	48.3	237	1	2
BUFFALO*	27	14	51.9	209	1	2
Season Totals	472	259	54.9	3724	26	25

PLAYOFFS

	Att	Comp	Pct	Yds	TD	Int
MIAMI†	31	21	67.7	230	2	0
Houston‡	30	18	60.0	219	2	1
Los Angeles§	21	14	66.7	309	2	3

LEGEND
Pittsburgh home games indicated by capitals.

Passing:

Att attempts
Comp completions
Pct percentage completed
Yds yards gained passing
LG longest gain passing
TD touchdowns passing
Sks quarterback sacks
Yds yards lost on sacks

Rushing:

Att attempts
Yds yards gained rushing
Avg average gain per attempt
LG longest gain rushing
TD touchdowns rushing

*Indicates Bradshaw as starting quarterback
‡AFC Championship Game

†AFC Playoff Game
§Super Bowl

1978

Opponent	Date	Att	Comp	Pct	Yds	LG	TD	Int	Sks	Yds	Att	Yds	Avg	LG	TD
			PASSING									**RUSHING**			
Buffalo*	9-3	19	14	73.7	217	38	2	1	0	0	3	−6	−2.0	−2	0
SEATTLE*	9-10	33	17	51.5	213	20	2	0	2	28	3	6	2.0	8	0
Cincinnati*	9-17	19	14	73.7	242	48	2	1	0	0	1	10	10.0	10	0
CLEVELAND*	9-24	32	14	43.6	208	37	1	2	1	8	2	27	13.5	17	0
New York Jets*	10-1	25	17	68.0	189	26	3	1	0	0	1	0	0.0	0	0
ATLANTA*	10-8	18	13	72.2	231	70	1	0	1	11	2	3	1.5	6	1
Cleveland*	10-15	21	10	47.6	175	36	2	0	3	22	1	0	0.0	0	0
HOUSTON*	10-23	33	17	51.5	226	42	2	1	1	11	2	26	13.0	−15	0
KANSAS CITY*	10-29	13	7	53.8	109	29	1	2	3	27	1	6	6.0	6	0
NEW ORLEANS*	11-5	23	15	69.6	200	29	2	1	0	0	2	4	2.0	5	0
Los Angeles*	11-12	25	11	44.0	125	36	1	3	1	10	1	2	2.0	2	0
CINCINNATI*	11-19	30	12	40.0	117	21	0	4	2	33	1	−3	−3.0	−3	0
San Francisco*	11-27	21	13	61.9	195	25	3	1	2	28	6	6	1.0	8	0
Houston*	12-3	25	11	44.0	97	34	1	1	2	23	3	−3	−1.0	—	0
BALTIMORE*	12-9	18	11	61.1	240	60	3	2	2	13	3	15	5.0	12	0
Denver*	12-16	14	10	71.4	131	25	2	0	1	9	0	0	0.0	0	0
Season Totals		368	207	56.3	2915	—	28	20	21	223	32	93	2.9	—	1

PLAYOFFS

Opponent	Date	Att	Comp	Pct	Yds	LG	TD	Int	Sks	Yds	Att	Yds	Avg	LG	TD
DENVER†		29	16	55.2	272	45	2	1	0	0	2	4	2.0	3	0
HOUSTON‡		19	11	57.9	200	29	2	2	0	0	7	29	4.1	13	0
Dallas§		30	17	56.7	318	75	4	1	4	27	2	−5	−2.5	1	0

1977

Opponent	Date	Att	Comp	Pct	Yds	LG	TD	Int	Sks	Yds	Att	Yds	Avg	LG	TD
			PASSING									**RUSHING**			
SAN FRAN*	9-19	23	12	52.2	164	29	1	0	3	31	4	20	5.0	16	0
OAKLAND*	9-25	32	16	50.0	268	43	1	3	5	51	2	18	9.0	13	0
Cleveland*	10-2	17	10	58.8	143	65	3	2	0	0	6	9	1.5	4	1
Houston	10-9	19	7	36.8	149	46	0	4	0	0	3	46	15.3	26	0
CINCINNATI*	10-17	9	6	60.0	117	40	0	0	3	30	3	−3	−1.0	−2	0
HOUSTON*	10-23	24	16	66.7	227	49	2	1	0	0	1	0	0.0	0	0
Baltimore*	10-30	26	11	42.3	234	50	1	5	2	15	3	37	12.3	17	0
Denver*	11-6	26	13	50.0	146	31	1	0	6	49	0	0	0.0	0	0
CLEVELAND*	11-13	21	13	61.9	283	39	3	0	2	18	0	0	0.0	0	0
DALLAS*	11-20	12	7	58.3	106	30	2	0	1	14	1	1	1.0	1	0
New York Jets*	11-27	28	10	35.7	143	37	2	1	2	19	3	3	1.0	6	0
SEATTLE*	12-4	21	13	61.9	158	26	1	1	1	1	4	40	10.0	16	2
Cincinnati*	12-10	39	20	51.3	246	26	0	1	1	7	0	0	0.0	0	0
San Diego*	12-18	17	8	47.1	139	46	0	1	0	0	1	0	0.0	0	0
Season Totals		314	162	51.6	2523	—	17	19	26	235	31	171	5.5	—	3

PLAYOFFS

Opponent	Date	Att	Comp	Pct	Yds	LG	TD	Int	Sks	Yds	Att	Yds	Avg	LG	TD
Denver†		37	19	51.4	177	60	1	3	0	0	4	21	5.3	11	0

Fractured left wrist: Houston 10-9

1976   PASSING   RUSHING

Opponent	Date	Att	Comp	Pct	Yds	LG	TD	Int	Sks	Yds	Att	Yds	Avg	LG	TD
Oakland*	9-12	27	15	55.6	253	39	1	1	2	11	2	1	0.5	3	0
CLEVELAND*	9-19	23	7	30.4	77	35	2	0	0	0	6	32	5.3	13	1
NEW ENGLAND*	9-26	39	20	51.3	291	47	1	0	3	44	6	42	7.0	14	0
Minnesota*	10-4	22	10	45.6	90	17	1	4	5	38	5	47	9.4	17	0
Cleveland*	10-6	18	10	55.5	75	26	0	1	4	49	2	17	8.5	10	0
CINCINNATI	10-17			Did	Not	Play									
N Y Giants	10-24			Did	Not	Play									
SAN DIEGO	10-31	19	9	44.0	104	19	1	1	1	16	1	1	1.0	1	1
Kansas City*	11-7	15	7	46.7	132	50	1	1	1	6	0	0	0.0	0	0
MIAMI*	11-14	2	0	0.0	0	0	0	0	0	0	3	37	12.3	15	0
HOUSTON	11-21			Did	Not	Play									
Cincinnati	11-28			Did	Not	Play									
TAMPA BAY	12-5	8	6	75.0	79	35	2	0	0	0	2	7	3.5	8	0
Houston*	12-11	19	8	42.1	76	21	1	1	0	0	4	35	8.8	15	1
Season Totals		192	92	47.9	1177	—	10	9	16	164	31	219	7.1	—	3

PLAYOFFS

Baltimore†		18	14	77.8	264	76	3	0	1	7	0	0	0	0	0
Oakland‡		35	14	40.0	176	32	0	1	3	11	1	4	4	4	0

Sprained right wrist: MIAMI 11-14

1975   PASSING   RUSHING

Opponent	Date	Att	Comp	Pct	Yds	LG	TD	Int	Sks	Yds	Att	Yds	Avg	LG	TD
San Diego	9-21	28	21	75.0	227	40	2	0	1	8	1	11	11.0	11	0
BUFFALO	9-28	8	3	37.5	69	59	0	1	4	38	3	7	2.3	4	0
Cleveland	10-5	8	7	87.5	151	45	1	0	1	5	1	−5	−5.0	−5	0
DENVER	10-12	26	16	61.5	191	43	2	0	1	1	3	15	5.0	15	0
CHICAGO	10-19	22	11	50.0	46	21	0	0	2	20	3	11	3.7	6	1
Green Bay	10-26	22	12	54.5	84	14	0	0	0	0	3	17	5.7	8	0
Cincinnati	11-2	24	13	54.2	164	37	2	2	3	34	2	3	1.5	2	1
HOUSTON	11-9	28	17	60.7	219	26	3	1	5	50	3	16	5.3	9	0
KANSAS CITY	11-16	24	16	66.7	204	42	2	1	2	23	1	2	2.0	2	0
Houston	11-24	16	13	81.3	168	25	1	2	3	29	5	26	5.2	11	0
New York Jets	11-30	22	9	40.1	120	44	2	0	2	12	3	56	18.3	27	0
CLEVELAND	12-7	25	11	44.0	135	20	2	0	4	37	3	30	10.0	11	0
CINCINNATI	12-13	23	13	56.5	149	24	1	1	1	21	3	19	6.3	9	1
Los Angeles	12-20	10	3	30.0	28	20	0	1	2	17	1	2	2.0	2	0
Season Totals		286	165	57.7	2055	—	18	9	31	295	34	210	6.2	—	3

PLAYOFFS

BALTIMORE†	12-27	13	8	61.5	103	34	0	2	3	27	3	22	9.2	13	1
OAKLAND‡	1-4	25	15	60.0	215	33	1	3	0	0	2	22	11.0	16	0
Dallas§	1-18	19	9	47.4	209	64	2	0	2	19	4	16	4.0	8	0

Cut hand: Cleveland 10-5
Strained knee tendon: Green Bay 10-26

1974

Opponent	Date	Att	Comp	Pct	Yds	LG	TD	Int	Sks	Yds	Att	Yds	Avg	LG	TD
				PASSING									RUSHING		
BALTIMORE	9-15			Did Not Play											
Denver	9-22			Did Not Play											
OAKLAND	9-29	2	1	50.0	11	11	0	1	0	0	2	18	9.0	26	0
Houston	10-6			Did Not Play											
Kansas City	10-13			Did Not Play											
Cleveland	10-20			Did Not Play											
ATLANTA*	10-28	21	9	42.9	130	29	0	2	1	10	9	16	1.8	9	1
PHILADELPHIA*	11-3	22	12	54.5	146	35	1	0	1	9	4	48	12.0	34	0
Cincinnati*	11-10	35	13	37.1	140	23	0	1	1	12	6	31	5.2	16	0
Cleveland	11-17			Did Not Play											
New Orleans*	11-25	19	8	42.1	80	31	2	2	2	18	9	99	11.0	33	1
HOUSTON*	12-1	20	6	30.0	60	31	1	1	3	38	2	2	1.0	2	0
New England*	12-8	16	10	62.5	86	17	1	1	2	17	1	6	6.0	6	0
CINCINNATI*	12-14	13	8	61.5	132	56	2	0	0	0	1	4	4.0	4	0
Season Totals		148	67	45.3	785	—	7	8	10	104	34	224	6.6	—	2
PLAYOFFS															
BUFFALO†	12-22	19	12	63.2	203	35	1	0	0	0	5	48	9.6	18	0
Oakland‡	12-29	17	8	47.1	95	23	1	1	1	14	3	15	5.0	8	0
Minnesota§	1-12	14	9	64.3	96	30	1	0	2	16	5	33	6.6	17	0

1973

Opponent	Date	Att	Comp	Pct	Yds	LG	TD	Int	Sks	Yds	Att	Yds	Avg	LG	TD
				PASSING									RUSHING		
DETROIT*	9-16	23	15	65.2	154	24	2	1	0	0	8	25	3.1	9	1
CLEVELAND*	9-23	14	5	35.7	140	49	1	1	3	20	2	16	8.0	10	0
Houston*	9-30	17	9	52.9	159	44	1	2	3	29	5	26	5.2	10	1
SAN DIEGO*	10-7	16	7	43.8	99	25	1	1	1	13	4	28	7.0	21	1
Cincinnati*	10-14	14	9	64.3	106	67	0	1	4	39	2	3	1.5	3	0
N Y JETS*	10-21	18	8	44.4	119	31	0	1	1	6	4	22	5.5	12	0
CINCINNATI*	10-28	7	3	42.9	37	22	0	1	2	8	1	4	4.0	4	0
WASHINGTON	11-5			Did Not Play											
Oakland	11-11			Did Not Play											
DENVER	11-18			Did Not Play											
Cleveland	11-25			Did Not Play											
Miami	12-3	35	14	40.0	117	19	2	3	4	27	2	3	1.5	2	0
HOUSTON*	12-9	20	11	55.0	117	24	2	4	2	15	3	8	2.7	5	0
San Francisco*	12-15	16	8	50.0	135	50	1	0	4	29	3	10	3.3	6	0
Season Totals		180	89	49.4	1183	—	10	15	24	186	34	145	4.3	—	3
PLAYOFFS															
Oakland†		25	12	48.0	167	—	2	3	1	9	3	9	3.0	5	0

1972   PASSING   RUSHING

Opponent	Date	Att	Comp	Pct	Yds	LG	TD	Int	Sks	Yds	Att	Yds	Avg	LG	TD
OAKLAND*	9-17	17	7	41.2	124	57	1	3	3	18	7	49	7.0	20	2
Cincinnati*	9-24	34	18	52.9	170	24	0	0	4	39	3	27	9.0	12	1
St. Louis*	10-1	40	25	62.5	229	38	1	1	2	20	7	35	5.0	20	1
Dallas*	10-8	39	12	30.8	166	32	0	1	3	24	4	32	8.0	11	0
HOUSTON*	10-15	19	9	47.4	70	16	1	0	3	24	7	34	4.9	8	1
NEW ENGLAND*	10-22	11	7	63.6	173	52	1	0	1	11	2	15	7.5	9	0
Buffalo*	10-29	17	9	52.9	93	17	1	1	0	0	2	6	3.0	5	1
CINCINNATI*	11-5	20	10	50.0	190	34	3	1	2	10	1	8	8.0	8	0
KANSAS CITY	11-12	20	8	40.0	92	36	0	3	2	12	5	34	6.8	11	0
Cleveland*	11-19	21	10	47.6	136	33	1	1	4	33	3	17	5.7	6	0
MINNESOTA*	11-26	19	7	37.8	93	43	1	1	1	7	6	28	4.7	9	1
CLEVELAND	12-3	17	9	52.9	162	78	1	0	1	9	5	27	5.4	12	0
Houston*	12-10	11	4	36.4	37	20	0	0	1	9	3	19	6.3	11	0
San Diego*	12-17	23	12	52.2	152	33	1	1	2	21	3	15	5.0	8	0
Season Totals		308	147	47.7	1887	—	12	12	29	237	58	346	6.0	—	7

PLAYOFFS

Opponent	Date	Att	Comp	Pct	Yds	LG	TD	Int	Sks	Yds	Att	Yds	Avg	LG	TD
OAKLAND†		25	11	44.0	175	60	1	1	3	31	2	19	9.5	12	0
MIAMI‡		10	5	50.0	82	25	1	2	1	9	2	5	2.5	3	0

1971   PASSING   RUSHING

Opponent	Date	Att	Comp	Pct	Yds	LG	TD	Int	Sks	Yds	Att	Yds	Avg	LG	TD
PRE-SEASON		98	54	55.1	749	55	8	4	6	51	21	108	5.1	20	1
Chicago*	9-19	24	10	44.7	129	42	0	4	0	0	2	4	2.0	4	0
CINCINNATI*	9-26	30	18	60.0	249	46	2	1	5	41	5	6	1.2	8	0
SAN DIEGO*	10-3	24	15	62.5	175	22	0	0	3	18	6	38	6.3	12	1
Cleveland*	10-10	27	12	44.4	126	22	2	1	3	24	3	15	5.0	12	0
Kansas City*	10-18	39	20	51.3	269	49	0	2	2	18	9	37	4.1	13	0
HOUSTON*	10-24	32	21	65.6	279	41	0	3	1	9	8	26	3.3	11	1
Baltimore*	10-31	35	20	57.1	187	31	1	1	3	32	3	12	4.0	9	2
CLEVELAND*	11-7	11	4	36.4	70	36	0	1	0	0	4	37	9.3	39	1
Miami*	11-14	36	25	69.4	253	30	3	2	4	34	2	5	2.5	4	0
N Y GIANTS*	11-21	20	12	60.0	75	19	1	0	1	15	1	11	11.0	11	0
DENVER*	11-28	17	6	35.3	68	31	0	0	3	25	3	16	5.3	9	0
Houston*	12-5	31	14	45.2	111	20	0	3	5	52	2	8	4.0	4	0
Cincinnati	12-12	13	6	46.2	105	40	2	0	0	0	2	2	1.0	2	0
LOS ANGELES*	12-19	34	20	58.8	163	20	2	4	3	19	3	30	10.0	25	0
Season Totals		373	203	54.4	2259	—	13	22	33	287	53	247	4.7	—	5

Opponent	Date	PASSING									RUSHING				
		Att	Comp	Pct	Yds	LG	TD	Int	Sks	Yds	Att	Yds	Avg	LG	TD
PRE-SEASON	(5)	102	52	51.0	663	53	3	5	8	70	17	105	6.2	24	1
HOUSTON*	9-20	16	4	25.0	70	46	0	1	2	10	3	20	6.7	15	0
Denver*	9-27	26	13	50.0	211	38	0	1	3	33	3	9	3.0	5	0
Cleveland*	10-3	29	13	44.8	207	67	0	3	7	78	4	44	11.0	22	1
BUFFALO*	10-11	12	3	25.0	24	18	0	0	1	12	2	18	9.0	16	0
Houston*	10-18	17	8	47.1	208	67	1	3	3	30	3	1	0.3	9	0
Oakland*	10-25	27	12	44.4	138	26	1	4	5	44	2	19	9.5	15	0
CINCINNATI*	11-2	12	4	33.0	40	20	0	0	0	0	3	15	5.0	5	0
N Y JETS	11-8			Did	Not	Play									
KANSAS CITY	11-15	19	8	42.1	74	22	1	3	1	10	3	30	10.0	15	0
Cincinnati*	11-22	19	8	42.1	101	18	0	3	0	0	0	0	0	0	0
CLEVELAND	11-29	9	4	44.4	197	81	2	0	1	9	5	49	9.8	20	0
GREEN BAY	12-6	20	3	15.0	110	87	1	4	0	0	3	14	4.7	10	0
Atlanta	12-13	12	3	25.0	30	71	0	2	2	16	1	14	14.0	14	0
Philadelphia	12-20	0	0	0.0	0	0	0	0	0	0	0	0	0	0	0
Season Totals		218	83	38.1	1410	—	6	24	25	242	32	233	7.3	—	1

BRADSHAW vs. OTHER NFL TEAMS

Regular Season

Team	G	Att	Comp	Pct	Yds	LG	TD	Int	Sks	Yds
Atlanta	3	51	25	49.0	391	70	1	4	4	37
Baltimore	4	108	61	56.5	910	62	7	10	8	69
Buffalo	5	83	43	51.8	612	59	4	5	6	58
Chicago	2	46	21	45.6	275	42	0	4	2	20
Cincinnati	18	410	213	52.0	2919	67	17	20	31	301
Cleveland	17	358	181	50.6	2810	81	25	13	35	325
Dallas	3	76	30	39.5	398	32	2	1	5	49
Denver	6	133	76	57.1	1014	65	7	2	14	117
Detroit	1	23	15	65.2	154	24	2	1	0	0
Green Bay	2	42	15	35.7	194	87	1	4	0	0
Houston	18	404	201	49.8	2708	67	19	31	40	372
Kansas City	7	159	83	52.2	1112	50	8	14	12	100
Los Angeles	3	69	34	49.3	316	36	3	8	3	27
Miami	3	73	39	53.4	370	30	5	5	4	34
Minnesota	2	41	17	41.5	183	43	2	5	6	45
New England	4	92	52	56.5	771	52	4	1	10	102
New Orleans	2	42	24	57.1	280	31	4	3	2	18
New York Giants	1	20	12	60.0	75	19	1	0	1	15
New York Jets	4	93	44	47.3	571	44	7	3	5	37
Oakland	5	105	51	48.6	794	57	4	12	15	124
Philadelphia	3	48	24	50.0	322	37	2	2	2	16
St. Louis	2	71	39	54.9	435	38	3	3	3	28
San Diego	7	163	90	55.2	1049	46	5	9	11	105
San Francisco	3	60	33	55.0	494	50	5	1	9	87
Seattle	2	54	30	55.6	371	26	3	1	3	29
Tampa Bay	1	8	6	75.0	79	35	2	0	0	0
Washington	1	27	15	55.6	311	65	4	1	1	7
Totals	129	2859	1474	51.6	19,918	87	147	163	232	2122

Post-Season

Team	G	Att	Comp	Pct	Yds	LG	TD	Int	Sks	Yds
Baltimore	2	31	22	71.0	367	76	3	2	4	34
Buffalo	1	19	12	63.2	203	35	1	0	0	0
Dallas	2	49	26	53.1	527	75	6	1	6	46
Denver	2	66	35	53.0	449	48	3	4	0	0
Houston	2	49	29	59.2	419	34	4	3	3	22
Los Angeles	1	21	14	66.7	309	73	2	3	0	0
Miami	2	41	26	63.4	310	25	3	2	2	19
Minnesota	1	14	9	64.3	96	30	1	0	2	12
Oakland	5	127	60	47.2	828	60	5	9	8	65
Totals	18	417	233	55.9	3508	76	28	24	25	198

SINGLE GAME CAREER HIGHS
Regular Season

Pass attempts: 44 (1979, vs. Cleveland)
Completions: 30 (1979, vs. Cleveland)
Yards passing: 364 (1979, vs. Cleveland)
Highest completion percentage: 87.5 (7 of 8, 1975, at Cleveland)
Longest completion: 87 yards (TD, to Dave Smith, 1970, vs. Green Bay)
Touchdown passes: 4 (1979, vs. Washington)
Interceptions: 5 (1979, at San Diego; 1977, at Baltimore)
Times sacked: 7 (1970, vs. Cleveland)
Rushing attempts: 9 (3 times, last time 1974, at New Orleans)
Yards rushing: 99 (1974, at New Orleans)
Longest run: 39 (1971, vs. Cleveland)

Post-Season

Pass attempts: 37 (1977, at Denver)
Completions: 21 (1979, vs. Miami)
Yards passing: 318 (1979, vs. Dallas)
Highest completion percentage: 77.8 (14 of 18, 1975, at Baltimore)
Longest completion: 76 (TD, 1975, vs. Baltimore)
Touchdown passes: 4 (1979, vs. Dallas)
Interceptions: 3 (4 times, last time 1980, vs. Los Angeles)
Times sacked: 4 (1979, vs. Dallas)
Rushing attempts: 7 (1979, vs. Houston)
Yards rushing: 48 (1974, vs. Buffalo)
Longest run: 25 (1980, vs. Houston)

STEELERS' SEASON RECORDS
(Excluding Playoffs)

Year	W	L	T	Year	W	L	T
1979	12	4	0	1974	10	3	1
1978	14	2	0	1973	10	4	0
1977	9	5	0	1972	11	3	0
1976	10	4	0	1971	6	8	0
1975	12	2	0	1970	5	9	0

COLLEGE CAREER RECORD
Louisiana Tech University

Year	Att	Comp	Pct	Yds	Td	Int
Freshman	81	34	41.9	404	0	3
Sophomore	139	78	56.1	981	3	10
Junior	339	176	51.9	2890	22	15
Senior	248	136	54.8	2314	14	14
Totals	807	424	52.5	6589	39	42